Presentation Pieces and Trophies

from the Henry Birks Collection of Canadian Silver

Presentation Pieces and Trophies

from the Henry Birks Collection of Canadian Silver

Ross Fox

National Gallery of Canada, Ottawa, 1985

PHOTO CREDITS

Rights to photographic materials used for reproduction – Except for the following figures, photographs have been supplied by the owners or custodians of the works reproduced; the courtesy of all is gratefully acknowledged:
Figs. 1, 15, 18, 19, 28 National Gallery of Canada,
Fig. 16 Charles A. Mason, St Andrews, N.B.,
Fig. 17 Royal Ontario Museum, Toronto,
Fig. 23 Henry Birks & Sons Limited, Montreal,
Figs. 25, 26, 27 Public Archives Canada (C-59193, C-65836, C-61430, respectively),
Fig. 29 Tom Scott, Edinburgh.

Every reasonable attempt has been made to identify the holders of rights of ownership in regard to reproductions. Errors or omissions will be corrected in subsequent reprints.

PRINTED IN CANADA

DESIGN: Carisse Graphic Design Ltd.

Canadian Cataloguing in Publication Data

Fox, Ross Allan C., 1945–

Presentation pieces and trophies from the Henry Birks Collection of Canadian Silver.

Issued also in French under title: Pièces honorifiques de la Collection Henry Birks d'orfèvrerie canadienne.

Includes index.

Bibliogr.: p.

ISBN 0-88884-517-0

1. Silverwork — Canada — History. 2. Silversmiths — Canada — History.   I. National Gallery of Canada.   II. Title.

NK7113 .Al F69 1985   739.2'3771   C84-097606-2

Jacket Cover/Frontispiece

One of a set of five pieces in a silver tea and coffee service presented in 1851 to Montreal businessman John Leeming, this teapot is the work of Montreal artist-designer James Duncan, engraver George Matthews, and silversmiths Peter Bohle and Robert Hendery. It stands 24.5 cm high. The set is part of the Henry Birks Collection of Canadian Silver in the National Gallery of Canada. See Chapter II, ''The 1850s: Background to a New Era,'' and figures 20 to 23.

Contents

Foreword

In December 1979, the distinguished Canadian firm of Henry Birks & Sons Limited announced the gift of its unique and priceless collection of Canadian silver to the National Gallery of Canada. The timing of the announcement highlighted a happy coincidence: as the firm of Henry Birks & Sons Limited neared the end of its centennial year, the National Gallery was about to celebrate its own one hundredth anniversary.

The Birks Collection began as the personal project of Henry Gifford Birks, grandson of the founder of the Birks firm. In 1936 he began to collect odd pieces by early Montreal silversmiths. Soon thereafter he conceived the idea of assembling examples of marks used on sterling silverware produced before 1899 by predecessors of the Birks silver factory in Montreal. Henry G. Birks soon realized that the art of early Canadian silversmiths had not received the recognition or protection it merited. Through fire or loss, melting down or removal from the country, much of it had already disappeared. To encourage research and the preservation of Canadian silver, he broadened his original plan and formed a permanent collection.

Today that collection of Canadian silver is the finest and most comprehensive in existence. It is composed of some 6 800 pieces of ecclesiastical, secular, and Indian trade silver made by craftsmen from the late seventeenth century to the present. In addition to Canadian silver, the collection also includes American, French, British, and British colonial pieces, as well as pieces from Russia, Germany, Denmark, and other countries. Almost all of this silver was collected in Canada – most at a time when little was known about the marks of Canadian silversmiths – in the sometimes justified hope that the works might prove to be Canadian. Whether made for export to Canada, brought by immigrants, or fashioned in this country, the pieces in the Birks Collection reveal not only the varied character of silver but also the special relationship of silver to social and cultural history.

It was always a Birks policy to lend parts of the collection to Canadian and international museums and to certain non-profit institutions for exhibition and educational purposes. Determination to preserve this important segment of Canadian heritage was combined with a desire to share the collection with the Canadian public. By placing the collection in the care of professionals at the National Gallery, the Birks firm felt that both objectives would be attained.

In the past four years, the National Gallery has devoted considerable effort to the Birks Collection. Ross Fox, Assistant Curator of Early Canadian Art, has been responsible for the collection. He has facilitated arrangements with institutions that have requested loans, some of them long-term. With his help, parts of the collection have travelled across the country and interested researchers have come to Ottawa to study the pieces. In 1981, he organized a major exhibition in Ottawa, *Heritage – The Henry Birks Collection of Canadian Silver*. The exhibition presented a selection of some two hundred pieces and was accompanied by a brochure describing the collection.

In March 1983 an exhibition of eighty-two "presentation" pieces from the Birks Collection, organized by Ross Fox, began a sixteen-month cross-country tour to eight institutions, accompanied by an illustrated issue of the Gallery's *Journal*. Details of that exhibition are given in Appendix III of this book.

"Presentation" silver, the subject of this volume, includes all those commemorative pieces donated by a benefactor for presentation to individuals in honour of some outstanding achievement – whether it be service to the community or backing a winning racehorse. These pieces are inscribed with historical names, sometimes engraved with scenes of long-vanished landmarks. It is the recording of such fascinating details of our social history as well as the history of presentation silver that Ross Fox has accomplished so thoroughly and sensitively in this book. As he explains in Chapter IV, the crafting of Canadian presentation silver reached its zenith in the second half of the nineteenth century, and it is this period that is best represented in the Birks Collection and that he has chosen to treat in this study, the first of its kind in Canada.

The National Gallery is grateful to Ross Fox for his commitment to the study and care of the Birks Collection. We trust his book on presentation silver will be only one of many studies to be done on the collection in the future.

To Henry Birks & Sons Limited we express special and deep appreciation for its generous gift, through the National Gallery, to all the people of Canada.

Joseph Martin, Director
National Gallery of Canada

Preface

This book was conceived and planned as a comprehensive study of a cohesive selection of works from the celebrated Henry Birks Collection of Canadian Silver.

Presentation silver, including trophies, seemed an especially fruitful theme for such a study. It provided an opportunity to examine one of the most fascinating and significant segments in the history of later nineteenth-century silver in Canada. The project also promised to offer a valuable body of datable material that could be used to resolve some problems in identifying common silver marks and to establish a tentative chronological framework for their use (see Appendix I).

Canadian presentation silver has never before been treated in a significant publication – nor for that matter has later nineteenth-century Canadian silver. I decided therefore to carry the project one step further and sketch a context for presentation silver. The result is an introduction to the history of presentation silver in Canada, from its beginnings until the early twentieth century. To accomplish this I had to interpose in the text, by way of illustration and discussion, a number of pieces of silver that do not belong to the Birks Collection. Nevertheless, the core of works derive from that collection; and in spite of the incorporation of other works, the text reflects a certain inevitable bias which concerns the nature of the Birks Collection itself. Originally envisaged as constituting works by the Montreal silversmithing predecessors of Henry Birks & Sons Limited, the scope was enlarged to include other Quebec silversmiths, and eventually others elsewhere in Canada, even though the latter are less plentiful and definitely underrepresented.

Necessary acknowledgements are numerous, and it is with warm gratitude that I remember all who have contributed to this publication. Above all I am indebted to Helena Ignatieff. As a former curator of the Royal Ontario Museum, Mrs Ignatieff has had a longtime interest in presentation silver, and it is to her that I owe the idea for this publication and the inspiration to carry it through. Harry M. Allice gave much generous and invaluable counsel, for which I am most grateful.

Mrs Ignatieff and Mr Allice kindly read the typescript and provided many useful comments. Also meriting special recognition are: Susan North, who assisted admirably with the preliminary research; Ruth Anne Labonté Fox, my wife, who helped with endless details; Honor de Pencier, who likewise provided much help and information, and reviewed my comments on marks; and Robert Fillion and Claude Lupien who did the splendid photography.

I also wish to thank all others who gave information, or of their time and energies. Among these are: L. Maxwell Taylor, Jocelyn A. Moss, Michael Pantazzi, Timothy R. Rees, Charles C. Hill, Orest M. Mazuryk, Maija Vilcins, Susan M. Hare, Edgar Andrew Collard, Warren Baker, Eric O.W. Hehner, Allan Raymond, John Bland, Luba Hussel, Mary Allodi, Claude Thibault, Norman Lowe, Thomas L. Gaffney, Nicole Cloutier, Thomas King, Pamela Wachna, Mrs G. Lebans, George C. Hendrie, Mrs V. Berry, Mrs M. Wainman-Wood, O.R. Macklem, Robert Derome, Christine Grant, Judith Tomlin, Gaétan Chouinard, Louise McNamara, Jean-René Ostiguy, Kathleen Slane, Elizabeth Wright, Victoria Baker, Mrs Terry Lightman, George R. Dalgleish, Ann Thomas, Provincial Library, Victoria, B.C., Public Archives and National Library of Canada.

To the staff of the National Gallery's Publications Division I owe special thanks. To Peter Smith, head of the division, who guided the project from the beginning; to Arnold Witty for providing technical know-how and, with Irene Lillico, coordinating the editing and production; to Lynda Muir and Norman Dahl, my English-language editors, who helped smooth and clarify my text; to Hélène Papineau, whose French-language adaptation of the manuscript has entailed not only steeping herself in the subject of presentation silver in her own language but also researching silver terminology in French; to Colleen Evans, who helped choose the photographs for the book and who managed their assembly; to Roy Engfield and Hélène Papineau, whose comprehensive index ends this work – to all these, and their support staff, I am profoundly grateful for their advice, criticism and, above all, encouragement.

Note on Identifying Marks

The form used in identifying pieces and distinguishing between makers and retailers, particularly in the figure captions, is one that has been adopted from some recent British silver publications. That is, when a mark on a piece of silver is recognized as belonging to a specific maker (silversmith or manufacturing silversmith), it is identified as such – for example, maker's mark of so-and-so. In the text it would be stated simply as *by* so-and-so. When marks are present for both a maker and a retailer, the identification is given as *by* so-and-so *for* so-and-so. When the only mark on a piece of silver is that of a retailer, it is identified as the mark of so-and-so. The latter also applies to situations of uncertainty – that is, if it is not known whether a mark signifies a maker or a retailer.

Unless otherwise stated, all works were made in Canada, and the medium is silver. Accession numbers for pieces from the various collections are given in parentheses. In photo captions, for example, the National Gallery accession numbers for the Birks Collection appear thus: Birks (24139). When inscriptions on pieces from the Birks Collection have been recorded in the text, original spelling and punctuation have been respected. The method used in dating individual works is set out in Appendix I.

Ross Fox
Ottawa

Chapter I

1 Presentation cup. Maker's mark of James Sutton and James Bult, London, England, 1782–83. Silver; 37.5 cm high. History Division, National Museum of Man, Ottawa (D-2437).

2 Teapot and stand. Maker's mark of Charles Hollinshed, London, England, 1806–07. Silver; 18.9 cm high (overall). McCord Museum, McGill University (M2615 and M2616).

1790–1850: The Early Years

Presentation silver is largely a phenomenon of the nineteenth century, whether in Canada or elsewhere in the Western World, although it has much deeper historical roots. Commemorative in character – in fact, often referred to as "testimonial" – such silver offered a highly suitable means for honouring a person with a tribute that was tangible, durable, portable, relatively valuable, frequently serviceable, and bearing an appropriately inscribed epigraph or dedication. Tributes of this kind were bestowed in acknowledgement of service or achievement, or they could be purely commemorative. They are affirmations of a collective and public nature on the one hand, or of an individual, private, and even intimate nature on the other, with many other possibilities in between. Silver trophies also have a long history, and their prevalence is approximately concurrent with that of presentation silver. As implied by their very name, they are prizes or awards for victories in competition, principally in sports. Again, their uses are manifold.

In general, presentation silver of this kind was especially esteemed in English-speaking countries, notably Britain and the United States, but it is by no means exclusive to them. This cultural taste is reflected in Canada where, from its first appearance, the custom is more readily identified with the English than the French-speaking community. Even those early examples wrought by francophone silversmiths were for the most part commissioned by anglophone clients and bear inscriptions in English.

One of the few pieces identifiable with the eighteenth century and with the early phase of British colonial rule after 1763 is a two-handled cup with cover (Fig. 1), the work of James Sutton and James Bult, with London (England) hallmarks for 1782–83. As demonstrated here, the earliest presentation silver was no doubt imported, and although an eighteenth-century Canadian example has yet to surface, presumably at least a few pieces were made by colonial silversmiths, even if rather modest in design. Most presentation silver continued to be imported until well past

the mid-nineteenth century and on into the twentieth. England was the dominant source in the early period.

The Sutton & Bult cup bears this inscription in Latin: *J: G: S: / Præ: Prov: Canada: Sup: / Alex: Mackenzie / Qui Princeps / Itinere Terrestri / Mare Pacificum / Indagavit / D: D: / 1794*. The event commemorated is Alexander Mackenzie's epoch-making transcontinental journey of exploration to the Pacific Ocean, completed in 1793. Mackenzie was the first European to traverse the full breadth of the North American continent, and in recognition of this feat he was knighted in 1802, two months after the publication of his *Voyages*.[1] The initials "J.G.S." of the inscription can signify none other than Colonel John Graves Simcoe, who was Lieutenant-Governor of Upper Canada from 1791 to 1796; this is also indicated by the words that follow the initials. Mackenzie visited the Lieutenant-Governor briefly at Newark (now Niagara-on-the-Lake) in September 1794 on his return east from the Pacific.[2]

This cup was likely presented in 1794, the year inscribed, and testifies that from the outset Simcoe comprehended the full import of Mackenzie's achievement and wished to honour him suitably. There is no question of a cup such as this being fashioned in Upper Canada at a time when colonization had just begun and silversmiths with adequate skills were lacking. In addition to its being English, the cup was actually made early in the preceding decade. Thus it might be surmised that Simcoe merely had an existing cup adapted for the occasion by having an appropriate inscription added. Covered cups of related design were plentiful in England during this period – urn-shaped with looped handles, and delicate bright-cut ornament of interlaced garlands and finely beaded edges. This cup fits firmly within the Neoclassic aesthetic.

Another later English import in the same general style is a teapot with stand by Charles Hollinshed (Fig. 2). As it bears Hollinshed's first mark, registered at the Assay Office at Goldsmith's Hall in London on 7 February 1807,[3] and as it also bears the date letter L

1

2

3

which expired in May of that same year, this teapot was likely fashioned sometime between those months. From the point of view of design it reflects the eclecticism of Regency Neoclassicism. All motifs are Neoclassic – including the narrow gadrooned edges of the lid and stand, the leaf surround and Greek fret of the lid, the acanthus leaves of the spout, the handle squared at the top, and the lion-paw feet of the pot. On the other hand, the profile of the body betrays an almost Egyptian aspect in its upper cavetto, perhaps drawing inspiration from Egyptian architecture. However, it is the overall form of the teapot itself that arrests attention. On first glance it summons to mind an imitation of an ancient, possibly Roman, cinerary urn or ossuary, when in reality it has no exact parallel in Antiquity. It is, however, related to general sarcophagal forms of a type found in English sepulchral art of the late eighteenth and early nineteenth centuries.[4] That the form is intended as funerary is confirmed in the small casket on a pedestal which is engraved on one side of the teapot and echoes it in its essentials, including the stand. The casket has a tabula inscribed with this epigraph: *John Paterson / Ob. 25 June 1806 / Æt. 74.*

Similar words appear on the outside edge of the teapot stand, clearly defining it as a memorial to John Paterson, who died on 25 June 1806 at seventy-four years of age. This theme is carried through in further inscriptions – for example, in the eulogy inscribed just below the casket in the lower part of the wreath reserve formed by two crossed branches. The inscription reads: *He was a Man eminently distinguished / through Life for the Rectitude of his Heart, / and Integrity of his Conduct, and no / less endeared to his Friends, by the / social Virtues of Benevolence / Sincerity, and Affection.* Inscribed on the other side of the teapot, as well as on its stand, in a lunette frame, is the dedication: *To / The HON^BLE JAMES McGILL Esqr / in Memory of a / Sincere Friend. / 1807.*[5]

James McGill is the Scottish-born Montreal merchant and philanthropist who made a fortune in the fur trade and founded McGill University. John Paterson, also a Scot, may have been a business agent of McGill's. His obituary in *The Gentleman's Magazine,* July 1806 (p. 680), describes him as "one of the oldest merchants in the Canada trade." He was based in London but died in Bristol, England.

While from the modern viewpoint the concept of such a memorial may seem slightly macabre, it is certainly not remote from early nineteenth-century sensibilities. Urns were the most commonly used forms for memorials of this type. However, to conceive an object such as a teapot as a memorial, especially when it is also intended for regular utilitarian use, certainly makes it an anomaly. Because of its extremely uncommon nature, it is probably safe to speculate that this teapot was made following specific instructions left by Paterson in a bequest. The McCord Museum has a covered urn (acc. no. M20292) by Benjamin Smith II and James Smith III, with London hallmarks for 1808–09, which was presented to McGill "In Testimony of the Esteem and Gratitude of an obliged Friend" who remains unidentified. Evidently this urn was the gift of a living rather than a deceased friend.

Race cups for equestrian competition are without a doubt among the earliest as well as the finest of silver trophies, and the custom of presenting them comes from England. An early mention of such a cup is that of the Montreal Jockey Club, valued at ten guineas and competed for on 7 August 1811.[6] Among the earliest surviving Canadian-made trophies are a series of small beakers awarded by the Montreal Florist Society in the period 1812–13. That at the Montreal Museum of Fine Arts is quite typical (Fig. 3). Consisting of a plain and thin-walled bell form, it has a moulded lip and low footring, and is the work of the Montreal silversmith Salomon Marion (1782–1830). The winner was "Mr. William Bell, for producing the best carnation, named Newlands Beauty of England. The second best flower was also produced by Mr. Wm. Bell, named Beell's [*sic*] Queen Charlotte."[7] The occasion was the 1812 annual show of carnations of the Montreal Florist Society. Bell also produced the finest carnation in 1815, but it is not known whether he received a prize that year.[8]

Another almost identical beaker by Marion at the Royal Ontario Museum (acc. no. 982.10.4) was awarded to John Teasdale at the annual show of auriculas and polyanthuses on 2 June 1812.[9] How many of these beakers were awarded and over how long a period is not known, although newspaper references indicate there were others. A visitor to Montreal in 1817, Joseph Sansom, noted: "There is here a

Society of Florists, who gave premiums, whilst I was at Montreal, for the finest specimens of ranunculuses and carnations.''[10]

The prototype for the Marion beakers is English, as is at least one other of those made for the Montreal Florist Society, now at the Musée du Québec (acc. no. A-60.230-0). By John Nickolds, this piece is somewhat puzzling because there is a discrepancy between the date of the inscription, 1813, and that of the London hallmarks, 1814–15. However, the inscription does agree with newspaper accounts of the event, such as that of the *Montreal Herald* of 24 May 1813 (p. 3): ''The Montreal Florist Society held a meeting on Thursday last at Mr. Dillon's Hotel for their annual show of Hyacinths, Auriculas, and Polyanthuses.... The prize was adjudged to Mr. Alex M'Kenzie gardner [*sic*] to John Molson, Esq. for producing the finest Hyacinth flower, named Prince Regent.'' The only conclusion to be arrived at is that there was a delay of a year before Mr McKenzie was actually given his prize.

Montreal was the largest metropolis and the chief commercial centre of Canada; hence a great deal of presentation silver is associated with that city. Salomon Marion was one of its principal silversmiths, and probably the most interesting from an artistic standpoint. In contrast to the subdued beakers of the type shown in figure 3, Marion was given an opportunity to display his considerable skills in a goblet that is now in the Birks Collection (Fig. 4). This is a very early Canadian-made presentation piece. Admittedly it too reproduces a fairly commonplace form; nevertheless, it is ornamented with narrow bands of delicately chased ornament and its lower cup is encased in a calyx of rayed leafwork, which hints at a virtuoso silversmith. The following dedication appears on the front of the cup, between an engraved ploughshare and harrow: *THIS CUP / is presented to / R^t. Gillespie Esqr / vice President of the / Montreal Agricultural / Society.* The dedication continues on the reverse side of the cup: *By the Farmers / of the Island of Montreal / as a token of respect for / Promoting the / AGRICULTURAL INTEREST / of the DISTRICT.*

Robert Gillespie was another prominent Montreal merchant and businessman involved in the fur trade, and like most he was a Scot. Born in Lanarkshire, he emigrated to Canada in 1800 and became a partner in

3

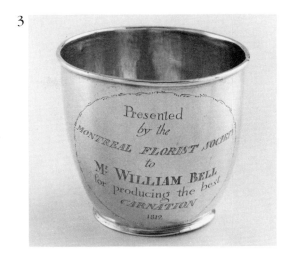

4

3 Trophy, Montreal Florist Society. Maker's mark of Salomon Marion, c.1812. Silver; 6.7 cm high. Montreal Museum of Fine Arts (949.Ds.7).

4 Presentation goblet, Montreal Agricultural Society. Maker's mark of Salomon Marion, c.1820–22. Silver, gilt lined; 19.5 cm high. Birks (24139).

5

5 Snuffbox. Maker's mark of Étienne Plantade, c.1821. Silver, gilt lined; 7.2 cm long. Birks (27765).

6 Two-handled cup. Maker's mark of Nelson Walker, c.1826. Silver; 25 cm high. The John and Eustella Langdon Collection of Canadian Silver, Royal Ontario Museum (L982. 18.1).

the firm of Parker, Gerrard and Ogilvy (afterwards Gillespie, Moffatt, and Company) of the North West Company. In 1822 Gillespie went back to England to take charge of the company's London offices. He never returned to Canada, although he was later a founder of the Bank of British North America.

The Montreal Agricultural Society was organized in 1817 and Robert Gillespie was among its founders. Its stated objectives were

> to contribute, by its efforts, to the advancement of the science of Agriculture... to recompense or reward industry, by the distribution of prizes in money, or in agricultural instruments, or by honorable distinctions, granted under certain conditions, to persons who shall have excelled in the cultivation of the produce of the earth, or in the rearing of animals, or in the manner of executing some of the multiplied and various labours of their profession.[11]

Gillespie was vice-president of the society in 1820 and 1822, and would therefore have received the goblet in that period, before his return to Britain.[12]

A snuffbox by Étienne Plantade (1777–1828)[13] of Montreal is the earliest Canadian presentation piece in the Birks Collection that can be positively dated (Fig. 5). As with the Marion goblet, it was acquired in England in 1937, but quite separately. The box is rectangular with rounded corners and hinged lid, and it is completely handwrought. Of somewhat naïve appearance, especially in the summary depiction of three steamboats on the lid, it nonetheless possesses a simplicity, a sturdiness and, above all, an integrity which separate it from so many of the mass-produced English examples of the period with their engine-turned ornament. Plantade is little known, except for some ecclesiastical pieces for the Roman Catholic Church which all show the same high qualities.

In the early nineteenth century the snuffbox was among the most commonplace of forms for both testimonials and trophies. The Plantade piece is inscribed: *Presented to Jacob Dorge Esq*^r. */ by Capt*^{ns} *Hall Brush & Seymour / as a token of their particular esteem / W··· Henry 24 March 1821*. The exact nature of this testimonial is not known. Dorge was a merchant

of the town of William Henry (the present-day Sorel, Quebec). In the year 1821 – and in that year only – William Hall, George Brush, and George E. Seymour were all masters of the steamboats *Quebec, Car of Commerce*, and *Telegraph*, respectively, the names of which are found on the flags of the steamboats engraved on the snuffbox. Thomas Torrance, the owner of these vessels, was the competitor of the famous Molson Line. William Henry was the wintering station for steamboats plying the St Lawrence from May until December, the usual navigation season on the river. The port, situated at the junction of the Richelieu and St Lawrence Rivers, eighty kilometres below Montreal, was also a stopping place on the way to Quebec City.[14]

Nelson Walker (1799–after 1855) of Montreal is responsible for a piece that can be characterized as one of the earliest-known Canadian examples of the two-handled cup (Fig. 6), a well-known form used primarily for presentation pieces or trophies. Appearing recently at auction in Britain, this cup is now at the Royal Ontario Museum.[15] In essence it reflects English types of the so-called campana (or thistle) shape of the early 1800s through the 1820s. It has two S-scroll handles with cast leaf grips, a narrow band of stamped repeat ornament at the waist of the cup, and a stamped collar of oak leaves for the stem. The swelling lower cup is encircled by vertical, slightly radiating lobes. This type of lobed treatment, although found in English silver for several decades, does not appear in Canadian secular silver until the 1820s and 1830s (cf. Fig. 13).

The inscription reads: *PRESENTED / With permission of Lieut. Col. M*^c*Gregor / to the Mess of the New Commi's*^d *Officers of the 70*th *Reg*^t */ by the Fire Assurance Comp*^s *and Citizens of Montreal / as a small acknowledgement of their uniform good / conduct in Garrison, and readiness to give / assistance on all occasions / of Fire. / Montreal / 25*th *May 1826*. Contrary to the date inscribed, the *Montreal Herald* of 3 May 1826 (p. 3) informs us that this cup had already been presented. The early presentation may have been occasioned by the impending departure of the 70th (or The East Surrey) Regiment of Foot from Montreal to a post elsewhere.[16] Lieutenant-Colonel Charles McGregor (or M'Grigor) was regimental commander in Montreal.[17]

5

6

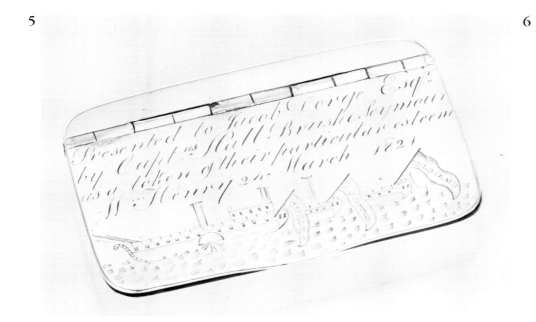

7 Beaker. Maker's mark of Nelson Walker, c.1834. Silver, gilt lined; 10.7 cm high. Birks (24118).

8 Covered urn. Maker's mark of John Bridge, London, England, 1830–31. Silver; 26 cm high. Le Château Ramezay, Montreal (CR5481).

Although Montreal had a Fire Society and a volunteer fire department, fire was a persistent problem. Here the military had an important role to play, as "Military aid at fires was probably the function of the garrison most appreciated by the townsmen."[18] The Walker cup certainly testifies to that.

Walker's role as a silversmith is not all that clear; he was also engaged in related endeavours such as engraver, jeweller, watch and clockmaker. A good deal of flatware with his mark exists, as do some table pieces. His mark also appears on a large presentation beaker in the Birks Collection, which is plain except for a moulded lip and footband (Fig. 7). The recipient was Captain John Neill of the ship *Robertson*, and the beaker was bestowed by passengers on a voyage from Greenock to Montreal "as a testimony of the high opinion they entertain of him, both as a sailor and gentleman."[19]

Transatlantic voyages of the period were arduous and hazardous, and when the ordeal was over, it was not infrequent for passengers to give their captain some token of their gratitude. Captain Neill sailed regularly on the run from Quebec City to Greenock, near Glasgow, Scotland. The *Robertson* set sail from Greenock 20 July 1834, arrived at Quebec City by mid-August, and at Montreal – the destination of the passengers – on 2 September. The presentation was made to Neill in Montreal about mid-September.[20]

In 1831 Captain Neill set a record by making three voyages that season from Greenock to Quebec City in the brig *Sophia*. In appreciation, a group of Montreal and Quebec City merchants presented him with a silver ewer, elaborately ornamented with foliate and vine motifs. Its whereabouts is not known, but as it has London hallmarks for 1832–33,[21] it must have been presented the year after Neill accomplished the feat.

Although Canadian silversmiths were engaged in making presentation plate during this period, most was still imported, particularly pieces of grand and ornate character. Thus the two-handled cup of Nelson Walker (Fig. 6) appears modest when compared with a covered urn by John Bridge (Fig. 8). Bridge was a former senior partner in the celebrated firm of Rundell, Bridge & Rundell, of London, purveyors to royalty and the aristocracy – he and Philip Rundell had been appointed Goldsmiths and Jewellers to King George III by 1797.

British North Americans were by no means unaware that the silver of this firm, or of its partners, even in these later years, was among the finest and most prestigious in the Empire.

The urn illustrated here is one of four by Bridge that were presented by Colonel John By to various contractors involved in building the Rideau Canal between Kingston and Bytown, present-day Ottawa. The front is inscribed: *THE GIFT / of L.ᵗ Colonel John By / Commanding Royal Engineer / OF THE RIDEAU CANAL. UPPER CANADA / To MESSʳˢ PHILLIPS AND WHITE / Contractors for the Lock and Dam at Black Rapids, / and three Locks, Dam and waste Wear, at Long Island / AS AN ACKNOWLEDGMENT of the ZEAL displayed by them / in the performance of their contracts, / and a TESTIMONIAL of the WORKS above-mentioned / having been executed to his complete satisfaction / PRESENTED / ON THE OPENING OF THE RIDEAU CANAL, / the 21ˢᵗ of August 1831*. In fact, the opening of the canal was postponed until May of the following year. Urns were also presented to Robert Drummond, John Redpath, and Thomas McKay.[22]

As a rule, colonial silversmiths were left with the trade in more modest wares, though without even a real monopoly of that. They were, however, much in demand for small cups, or children's cups, which are the most plentiful of types falling under the broad typological umbrella of presentation silver. While such cups exist early in the century, they really come into fashion only by the 1830s, and even then they are for the most part traditional and pedestrian in design. Figures 9 and 10 present two mugs by Peter Bohle (1786–1862) of Montreal. One has plain tapered sides, applied base and lip bands, and a scrolled handle; the other is quite similar, only octagonal in section. Both reproduce later eighteenth-century English models. The latter is engraved on the side: *F A McK / from / L Beaubien*. The McK may signify McKenzie, as this mug descended in the McKenzie family, former seigneurs of Saint-Canut, Quebec.

The earliest of the small presentation cups in the Birks Collection (Fig. 11) is by Laurent Amiot (1764–1839), with an inscription that reads: *From J.B. to his Cousin / Helen Scott Black / Quebec 4ᵗʰ December / 1817*. Quebec City, the other metropolis

7

8

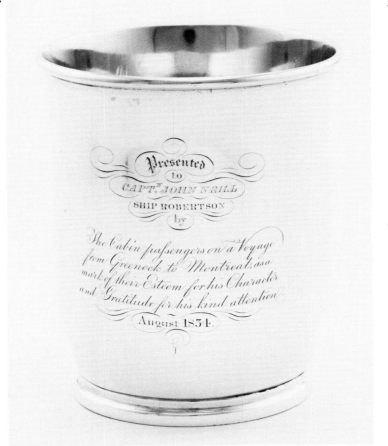

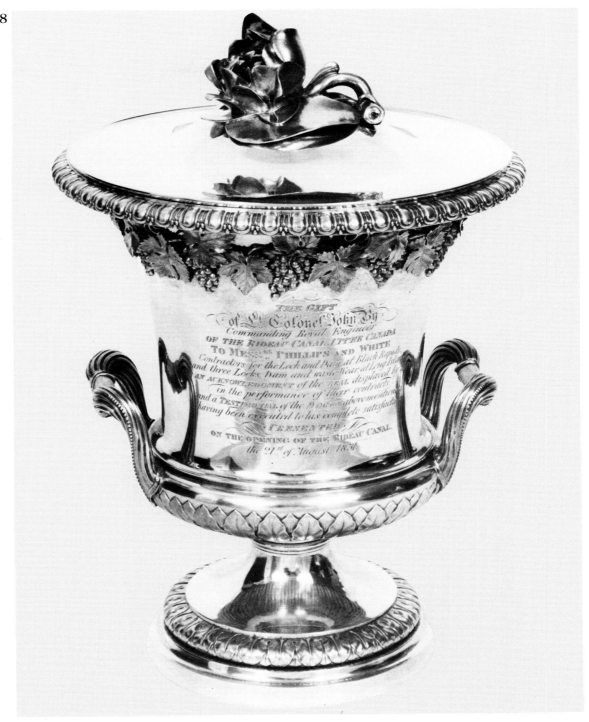

9 Mug. Maker's mark of Peter Bohle, c.1840–50. Silver; 8.8 cm high. Birks (24086).

10 Mug. Maker's mark of Peter Bohle for George Savage & Son, c.1840–50. Silver; 9.5 cm high. Birks (25204).

11 Child's cup. Maker's mark of Laurent Amiot, c.1817. Silver; 7.5 cm high. Birks (24141).

9

10

11

of Lower Canada, is where Laurent Amiot had his workshop. Amiot can lay claim to the title of consummate Canadian silversmith of the nineteenth century, although he does have a rival in Salomon Marion. Amiot excelled in ecclesiastical plate and executed many fine table pieces. Yet his presentation works are few in number and rarely attract interest. Another Amiot presentation piece is an ecuelle (or two-handled porringer) with cover (Fig. 12) – exceptional only in that it is not a form normally used in commemorative works. As is characteristic of so much of Amiot's œuvre, its overall effect depends on taut, highly burnished surfaces, relieved only by a simple ring-handle and two fluted palmette-form handles.

This ecuelle is a traditional French-Canadian (and French) vessel and is among the most common of silver forms in Canada in the eighteenth century. Those with palmette-form handles usually date to the third quarter of the century. By the beginning of the nineteenth century this vessel type was outmoded, although many examples were still to be found among household silver. The only feature that identifies this Amiot piece as having a significance beyond the utilitarian is an abbreviated inscription which is repeated on the cover and bowl: *From / WHB / to / MC.* These initials remain unidentifiable, but the ecuelle is part of a small group of silver pieces in the Birks Collection that come from the Coffin family of Quebec, descendants of John Coffin, a Loyalist from Boston who moved to Quebec City in 1775.

Perhaps the most captivating of Amiot's testimonials, if only anecdotally, is a ewer at the residence of the Roman Catholic Archbishop of Quebec (Fig. 13). The piece is stout and pyriform, its lower body enveloped by vertical lobes which are mirrored in the gadroons of the foot. The type is English from earlier in the century. Engraved on the upper body is a scene of a sailing ship amid high waves. On the opposite side is this lengthy epigraph: *Tribut de respect et de reconnoissance / OFFERT / par les propriétaires et assureurs du / BRIG. ROSALIND DE LONDRES, CAPT. BOYLE, / au / Rev.d Messire Asselin Ptre. Curé de St. Louis / DE L'ISLE AUX COUDRES / pour avoir / par son Exemple engagé ses paroissiens / à aider à sauver le Vaisseau et sa / Cargaison jetés par les glaces sur cette Isle le 27 Nov. 1832 / et pour / ses bontès envers les naufragés pendant / LEUR SEJOUR SUR L'ISLE.*

While departing from Quebec City in late November 1832, a number of ships became trapped in ice floes on the lower St Lawrence River. One of these, the *Rosalind*, was forced aground on the southeast shore of Isle-aux-Coudres. The local parish priest, the Reverend Charles-Joseph Asselin, organized his parishioners to save the vessel and its cargo.[23] As an expression of gratitude, the owners of the *Rosalind* arranged in the winter of 1833 for "£60 to be appropriated for the Church of the island, and as a testimonial to the Curate, Mr. Asselin."[24] It is somewhat out of the ordinary that the commission was awarded to a Canadian silversmith and not an English one, as the vessel's owners were based in London.

François Sasseville (1797–1864) of Quebec City is the maker of another tribute to a parish priest, a cruet tray (Fig. 14), which was given to the Reverend Patrick McMahon by his parishioners in 1846. McMahon was pastor of St Patrick's congregation in Quebec City from 1828 until his death in 1851, and he directed the building of its first church, dedicated in 1833. In effect an Irish national church, St Patrick's congregation, toward the end of McMahon's pastorate, numbered about 10 000, or almost a quarter of the city's population.[25] Sasseville, a francophone, attended McMahon's church, which may partially explain how he came to make the cruet tray.

The function of a cruet tray is twofold. It was intended to carry two cruets, one for the water, the other for the wine used in the celebration of the Eucharist of the Roman Catholic Church. The tray also served as a lavabo for the ritual washing of the fingers by the priest during the same celebration. In nineteenth-century Canada, cruets were customarily made of silver, as was the tray; consequently they were fashioned as a set. When the cruets became separated from the Sasseville tray is not known, but no doubt they existed.

Sasseville served his apprenticeship under Laurent Amiot and became his successor when the latter died in 1839. Thereafter Sasseville dominated the craft in Quebec City, but his presentation pieces are few. Most of his clientele were parishes or individual ecclesiastics.

Outside of Lower Canada, there were other silver-

12

13

14

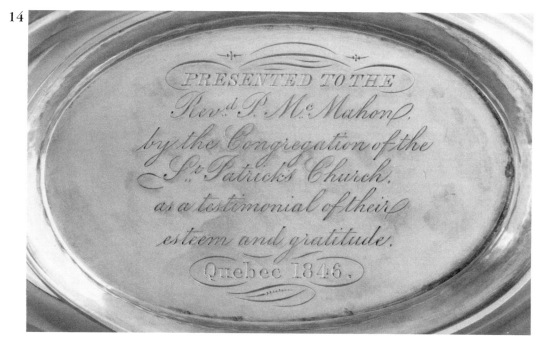

smiths engaged in making presentation plate.

Halifax was the centre of silver-crafting in Atlantic Canada. There were also silversmiths elsewhere, in Saint John, Charlottetown, New Glasgow, Truro, and so on, but flatware was their overwhelming if not almost exclusive commodity. Peter Nordbeck is the pre-eminent silversmith of the region. Born in Germany in 1789 and trained there, he spent a few years in the West Indies before going to Halifax in 1819, where he plied his craft until his death in 1861. The quintessence of Nordbeck's œuvre is exemplified in a goblet-form trophy for the Halifax Yacht Club (Fig. 15).[26] The cup is an undulating bell shape with delicately chased oak leaves enfolding the underside like a calyx. This combination of fluid lines, chased-work, and highly burnished surfaces imparts a gentle grace and elegance. A gartered medallion reserve, which is engraved midway up the cup, encloses this epigraph: *JOHN W. GORDON, R.E. / to / ROBERT STORY, ESQ^R.* The following is engraved on the garter: *In Token of his Success in the THISTLE, H.Y.C. Regatta, August 1837.*

The first regatta of the newly formed Halifax Yacht Club was held on 31 August 1837, although Halifax had been the site of organized yachting regattas as early as 1826.[27] The Halifax *Novascotian* of 6 September 1837 (p. 282) sums up the event to which the Nordbeck goblet pertains: "Second Class, first prize $30, Lieut. Gordon's (R.E.) Thistle; second, $30, Lieut. Craig's (R.N.) Timothy."

As it turns out, this newspaper account is not quite correct, for Robert Story, and not John Gordon, was the owner of the *Thistle*, as indicated by the inscription on the cup. It is common throughout the nineteenth century for a newspaper to record a prize solely in terms of its cash value, without distinguishing between a purse, trophy, or whatever. In this case only the existence of the trophy itself supplies the evidence of the precise nature of the prize. Thus newspaper accounts alone are an unreliable source in estimating the actual prevalence of silver trophies during any given period in that century.

John William Gordon was in fact the presenter of the Nordbeck goblet. A lieutenant in the Corps of Royal Engineers, and later major-general, he was stationed in Halifax at this time. The recipient, Robert Story, was

15

12 Ecuelle with cover. Maker's mark of Laurent Amiot, c.1800–35. Silver; 29.7 cm long. Birks (24015).

13 Ewer. Maker's mark of Laurent Amiot, c.1833. Silver; 27.3 cm high. Archevêché de Québec.

14 Cruet tray, detail of underside. Maker's mark of François Sasseville, c.1846. Silver; 20.3 cm long. Birks (24146).

15 Trophy, Halifax Yacht Club. Maker's mark of Peter Nordbeck, c.1837. Silver; 20.3 cm high. Private collection.

a Haligonian, and longtime member of the Halifax Yacht Club. Another almost identical goblet by Nordbeck was presented by Lady Campbell, wife of Sir Colin Campbell, Lieutenant-Governor of Nova Scotia from 1833 to 1840, and the "Ladies of Halifax" at the Halifax Regatta of 17 August 1836.[28]

Although plate was being fashioned in the Maritime colonies in the early nineteenth century, it accounted for only a small fraction of that actually used by the population. Instead there was an almost inordinate dependence on imports, much more so than in Lower Canada. Identifying these imports is not always an easy task. Most early Canadian plate is not inscribed, and, when over the years it eventually becomes disassociated from its original context, almost invariably the history of such pieces is lost.

Fortunately, presentation pieces and trophies are often an exception. Such is a trophy by Paul Storr with London hallmarks for 1814–15 (Fig. 16). An inscription under the lid reveals onetime ownership by Colonel Nehemiah Marks of St Stephen, New Brunswick. Marks's father, of the same name, was a Connecticut Loyalist who settled in New Brunswick in 1783. Marks himself was a prominent horse-breeder and horseman, and a longtime participant in equestrian competitions throughout the Maritimes until his death in 1855. According to oral tradition, Marks won the Storr cup for flat racing on the Halifax Common.[29] An inscription on the front reads: *Won by / DESDEMONA / 1837 / & / HUMBUG / 1838.*

Halifax has yet to be confirmed as the location of this event. The Halifax *Novascotian* of 13 December 1837 (p. 397) reports that the winner of the cup at the Halifax races in 1837 was a thoroughbred filly named Angelica owned by a Captain Broderick. On the same page is the notice: "Halifax Races. At a General Meeting of the Turf Club, held this day, it was resolved that a cup shall be received from England, to be run for as heretofore, at the Races in 1838." The *Novascotian* of 6 September 1838 (p. 286) relates further that the winner of that cup was again the horse Angelica, now owned by Colonel Snodgrass. It does not seem likely that the Storr cup has anything to do with either of these meets. Possibly it was competed for elsewhere, even in New Brunswick or Prince Edward Island.

Nonetheless, Colonel Marks is known to have entered the Halifax races on numerous occasions. These races were held under the auspices of the Halifax Turf Club, beginning in 1825, and continued every year for most of the century. Flat racing has an even older if more sporadic history in Nova Scotia and Atlantic Canada, but the years from 1825 to 1845 were the heyday for the sport in Halifax. It is also worth noting that the introduction of steeplechasing to this region, whether the hurdle steeplechase or the cross-country steeplechase, predates that in central Canada or the United States. A hurdle steeplechase is recorded at Saint John, New Brunswick, as early as 1836.[30] As there were many avid horsemen among the military as well as the local gentry, stakes for these meetings were often fairly substantial and included silver cups.

The Storr cup undoubtedly represents another case of an older piece of silver being reused, or rededicated, at a later period. Its original function is not known. The ornament is appropriate to a trophy, consisting of a frieze of entwisted clover and oak leaves below the rim, and a large centrally disposed laurel wreath framing the inscription. The cover, or at least the horse finial, has the appearance of a later addition. The form itself, that of a Classical calyx krater, is familiar in English silver of the period and was used, among other things, for presentation urns (cf. Fig. 8), trophies, and often wine coolers.

Toronto silversmiths provide the only known examples of the krater form being wrought in Canada. In general the circumstances under which the craft existed in Upper Canada differed little from those in the Atlantic region, and indeed most plate was imported. Toronto was the focus of activity, although silversmiths were also to be found in Kingston, Sandwich (now Windsor), Hamilton, and other centres. However, it must also be called to mind that in the first quarter of the century the province was still in the pioneering stage of development, lacking the long history of settlement of either Lower Canada or Nova Scotia.

Henry Jackson (active c.1837–1865) of Toronto was the craftsman of a splendid presentation urn of krater form (Fig. 17). With high and rather narrow neck, and two obliquely projecting scroll-handles, it does not adhere to Classical Greek models as does the Storr trophy above; rather, it is more attuned to slightly later ones, possibly even from South Italy. While in general

16
17

16 Trophy. Maker's mark of Paul Storr, London, England, 1814–15. Silver, gilt; 43 cm high. Collection of Mrs M. Wainman-Wood, St Andrews, New Brunswick.

17 Urn. Maker's mark of Henry Jackson, c.1838. Silver; 37.5 cm high. Upper Canada College, Toronto.

18 Trowel with turned wooden handle. Maker's mark of William Stennett, c. 1844. Silver; 29.9 cm long. The Market Gallery, City of Toronto Archives (14.1).

19 A six-light centrepiece and mirror plateau. Maker's mark of Edward, Edward Jr, John and William Barnard of Edward Barnard & Sons, London, England, for D.C. Rait, Glasgow, Scotland, 1842–43. Silver; 83 cm high. History Division, National Museum of Man, Ottawa (D-2439).

18

the urn imitates English taste, the exceptionally swollen lobes of the lower body have their nearest parallel in American silver of the period. Every second lobe is also chased with a generalized acanthus leaf. Otherwise there is a distinct sparsity of ornament, which might rightly be construed as the Canadian adjunct to the design. The plinth, which is square in section and has an outer casing of silver, bears this epigraph on one side: *J.H. HARRIS S.T.P. / Coll. U.C. Præsidi dignissimo. / Præceptoris grave munus deposituro.*

The dedication continues on the other side and affirms that the urn was presented to the Reverend Dr Joseph Hemington Harris on his resignation as principal of Upper Canada College, Toronto, on 1 April 1838. Harris, an Anglican priest, was the first principal of this prestigious private school from its foundation in 1829. He received the urn from his students; the masters gave him a silver inkstand.[31]

William Stennett is another silversmith who made a similar urn – this time more truly a Classical krater, and again for an Anglican clergyman. This urn was presented to the Reverend Dr Joseph Hudson: *As a memorial of that affection and esteem / which his faithfulness as the pious Clergyman, / The kind Friend of the Poor, / and upright member of Society / Daily increased while he Continued / Their assistant minister, / York, Upper Canada / 12th June 1833.* The presenters were the members of the congregation of St James's Church, Toronto. Some time ago this urn was repatriated from Scotland and is now in the possession of the Cathedral Church of St James.[32]

Stennett, an Englishman, was working in Bermuda in 1813, and by the end of the decade, he was in Kingston, Upper Canada. In 1829 he moved to Toronto, where he appears in records as late as 1846. A trowel by him (Fig. 18) is inscribed in this manner: *Presented / to the / Hon. H. Sherwood, / Mayor of Toronto / on laying the / Corner Stone / of the / New Market Buildings, / 4th September 1844, / By / Thomas Young / and / Daniel McDonald, / Contractors / for erecting the same.* This implement is an example of an extremely early Canadian ceremonial trowel. Most date to the next half century. Moreover, the fact that the buildings referred to above housed the new (second) Toronto City Hall, as well as a market, gives the trowel an added historical significance.[33]

Contrary to what these many fine specimens of workmanship by Canadian silversmiths might imply, a great deal of silver was still being imported by the 1840s. This applies as well to presentation pieces, and above all to the more sumptuous among them. An example of such, at least from a colonial viewpoint, is a centrepiece (Fig. 19) by Edward Barnard & Sons of London for the retailer, D.C. Rait, silversmith and jeweller in Glasgow, Scotland. Fundamentally a testimonial to William Morris as a lay leader in the Church of Scotland, it also acknowledges the role of Morris as a champion of that church's claims to a share in the Clergy Reserves of Upper Canada.

The reserve system was instituted by the *Constitutional Act* of 1791 and provided that public lands be allocated for the support of a Protestant clergy. As a consequence, one-seventh of all granted lands were set aside for that purpose. The Church of England (or Anglican Church) was at the outset the sole beneficiary, as it alone was accorded the privileges of a state religion. Within several decades, however, the Church of Scotland in Canada initiated claims for a share of these lands, arguing that by the Act of Union between England and Scotland it was as much an established church as the Church of England. In effect, they were seeking a status of co-establishment in Upper Canada. This challenge was of a protracted and highly polemical nature, and the delegated spokesman of the challengers for the duration was William Morris, a wealthy merchant from Brockville (and Perth), Upper Canada, who was born in Paisley, Scotland. Morris was a Member of the Legislative Assembly (1821–1836), the Legislative Council of Upper Canada (1836–1841) and the Legislative Council of United Canada (from 1841). He also served as Receiver-General of United Canada (1844–1846) and President of the Executive Council (1846–1848).

The interests of the Church of Scotland, and those of the various other Presbyterian bodies, were finally secured by the *Clergy Reserves Act* of 1840, which in principle acceded to their claims. The Church of England, with adherents numbering 20 per cent of the population, was given 42 per cent of the reserves; the Church of Scotland, with almost another 20 per cent of the population, was given 21 per cent. The remainder was left for later division, and would even-

19

17

tually be granted to Roman Catholics and Wesleyan Methodists.[34]

Much of the success of the claimants stemmed from the indefatigable representations of Morris to the British Colonial Office. Acknowledgement of this achievement and expressions of gratitude appear in a prolix epigraph on the pedestal of the centrepiece, the last part of which records: *And as the Delegated Agent / TO GREAT BRITAIN / OF THE / Presbyterians of Canada / TO PROTEST AGAINST THE INJUSTICE TO THEM / AND THE DANGER TO THE EMPIRE / OF THE ATTEMPT IN CANADA / To wrench from the Church of Scotland / her Ecclesiastical Equality and Rights / AND TO DEGRADE HER IN THE BRITISH COLONIES / From her Constitutional standing and use / AS A / National Establishment.*

The centrepiece was presented to Morris in July of 1843 "by Scotchmen, and other Members of the Presbyterian Church of Canada, in connexion with the Church of Scotland,"[35] and it has London hallmarks for 1842–43. Consisting of a candelabrum on a mirror plateau, the ornament is suitably emblematic. The central column, on a block pedestal, is surmounted by a statuette of John Knox with a Bible clasped in his right hand. The predominant motif is the Scotch thistle, as in the candle sockets which are cast as thistle flowers and the drip pans as small clusters of thistle leaves. A thistle vine also encircles the lower shaft of the column. In addition, the sides of the plateau are overlaid with grape vines. All ornament is oxidized as , are the flutes of the column. The profusion of thistle ornament is strongly symbolic. Especially after the English conquest and subjugation of Scotland in the early eighteenth century, the forbidding thistle became a popular symbol of the integrity of the Presbyterian Church and Scottish nation against the intrusive Sassenach. Overall the design betrays an incipient Victorian partiality for ostentation and ornamentation. It will be a couple of decades before a Canadian silversmith will attempt anything of such amplitude, either in scale or richness.

Notes

1. See W.K. Lamb, ed., *The Journals and Letters of Sir Alexander Mackenzie* (Toronto: Macmillan of Canada, 1970), p. 36.
2. Ibid., p. 23.

3. A.G. Grimwade, *London Goldsmiths 1697–1837: Their Marks and Lives* (London: Faber and Faber, 1976), p. 36 (no. 331).
4. J. Physick, *Designs for English Sculpture 1680–1860,* exhibition catalogue (London: Victoria and Albert Museum, 1969), passim.
5. This same inscription is found on the stand. See D.B. Webster et al., *Georgian Canada: Conflict and Culture 1745–1820,* exhibition catalogue (Toronto: Royal Ontario Museum, 1984), p. 144.
6. *Montreal Gazette,* 12 Aug. 1811, p. 1.
7. *Canadian Courant* [Montreal], 27 July 1812, p. 3.
8. *Montreal Gazette,* 5 Aug. 1815, p. 3.
9. *Montreal Herald,* 30 May 1812, p. 3; 6 June 1812, p. 3.
10. *Travels in Lower Canada* (1820; rpt. Toronto: Coles Publishing Company, 1972), p. 73.
11. *Montreal Herald,* 13 Sept. 1817, pp. 2, 3; 8 Nov. 1817, p. 2.
12. T. Doige, *An Alphabetical List of the Merchants, Traders and Housekeepers, Residing in Montreal,* 2nd ed. (Montreal: James Lane, 1820), p. 31; *Montreal Herald,* 26 Jan. 1822, p. 3.
13. Archives nationales du Québec, Montreal, Registers of Notre-Dame de Montréal (Church), indicate Étienne-Clément Plantade was born 19 September 1777, which presumably refers to the silversmith. However, the registers of the same church state that "Étienne Leplantade orfèvre" died 26 September 1828 at fifty-four years of age. An obituary in the *Quebec Gazette,* 2 Oct. 1828 (p. 3), gives the same information. Louis Carrier, "Silver of French Canada" (unpublished typescript), gives 1777 as the year of birth. However, the parents were married 3 May 1773, so it is just possible the silversmith was born earlier.
14. McGill University, McLennan Library, Department of Rare Books and Special Collections, John Molson and Son Papers, Bills of Lading, 1821, etc.; K. Jenkins, *Montreal, Island City of the St. Lawrence* (Garden City, N.Y.: Doubleday & Company, Inc., 1966), p. 252; *Montreal Herald,* 2 May 1821, p. 1.
15. Sotheby's (London), Sale, 19 July 1982, lot 30.
16. *Montreal Herald,* 27 May 1826, p. 3; *Montreal Gazette,* 29 May 1826, p. 2.
17. He was stationed in Canada from approximately November 1813 until June 1827. The *Army Lists* (London, The War Office) consistently spell his surname as M'Grigor. The same form is given in correspondence at Public Archives Canada, Military "C" Series.
18. E.K. Senior, *British Regulars in Montreal: An Imperial Garrison, 1832–1854* (Montreal: McGill-Queen's University Press, n.d.), p. 134.
19. *Montreal Gazette,* 20 Sept. 1834, p. 2.
20. Ibid.
21. 30.5 cm high, it was sold in May 1938 by Henry Birks & Sons, Hamilton, Ontario. National Gallery of Canada, Curatorial Archives. Also *Montreal Herald,* 22 Sept. 1834, p. 2.
22. J.D. Stewart and I.E. Wilson, *Heritage Kingston,* exhibition catalogue (Kingston, Ont.: Agnes Etherington Art Centre, 1973), p. 156; N. and H. Mika, *Bytown: The Early Days of Ottawa* (Belleville, Ont.: Mika Publishing Company, 1982),

p. 112. Re. Phillips see discussion of Fig. 37.

23. *Quebec Gazette*, 3 Dec. 1832, p. 2.

24. *Quebec Gazette*, 12 Apr. 1833, p. 3. Also see E.A. Jones, "Old Church Silver in Canada," *Transactions of the Royal Society of Canada*, 3rd ser., XII, sect. 2 (1918), pp. 144–145; R.-É. Casgrain, *Histoire de la paroisse de l'Ange-Gardien* (Quebec: Dussault & Proulx, 1902), pp. 271–272.

25. J.A. Gallagher, "St. Patrick's Parish – Quebec," *The Canadian Catholic Historical Association* (1947–48), pp. 72–75.

26. H. Piers and D.C. Mackay, *Master Goldsmiths and Silversmiths of Nova Scotia and Their Marks* (Halifax, N.S.: The Antiquarian Club, 1948), pp. 24, 27–28.

27. P.L. Lindsay, *A History of Sport in Canada, 1807–1867*, Ph.D. Thesis (University of Alberta, 1969), p. 169.

28. R.H. Hubbard and J.-R. Ostiguy, *Three Hundred Years of Canadian Art*, exhibition catalogue (Ottawa: National Gallery of Canada, 1967), pp. 52–53.

29. B.J. Christie, "Flat Racing in Nova Scotia: Testing Ground for Horses of Stamina and Quality (Part Two)," *The Occasional*, VII (Spring 1982), p. 24.

30. B.J. Christie, "Flat Racing in Nova Scotia: Testing Ground for Horses of Stamina and Quality (Part Three)," *The Occasional*, VII (Fall 1982), pp. 18, 21–23.

31. R.B. Howard, *Upper Canada College 1829–1979* (Toronto: Macmillan of Canada, 1979), p. 29.

32. H. Ignatieff, "Ontario Silversmiths," *Canadian Collector*, VI (May 1971), pp. 59–60; Webster et al., *Georgian Canada*, pp. 40, 202.

33. *The Patriot* [Toronto], 6 Sept. 1844, p. 2; *The Globe* [Toronto], 10 Sept. 1844, p. 3; W. Dendy, *Lost Toronto* (Toronto: Oxford University Press, 1978), pp. 48–52.

34. J. S. Moir, *The Church in the British Era: From the British Conquest to Confederation* (Toronto: McGraw-Hill Ryerson Limited, 1972), pp. 60–62, 113–116, 124–125.

35. *Montreal Gazette*, 15 July 1843, p. 2.

Chapter II

The 1850s: Background to a New Era

The history of Canadian silver enters a hiatus in the 1840s. By the end of the decade, Canadian silversmiths were making very little hollow ware for the table – the overwhelming commodity was flatware. Of course, several silversmiths in Montreal and Quebec City still continued to specialize in work for the lucrative ecclesiastical sector, almost exclusively for the Roman Catholic Church. Not that Protestants did not use silver vessels in their churches; they did, but they imported most of their communion plate. The 1850s mark a transitional period. Towards the end of the decade, at least in Montreal, the crafting of silver for secular purposes enjoyed a resurgence that continued throughout the century. Of greater significance for this study is the fact that presentation pieces and trophies form a large percentage of the more interesting and original works of the period.

The new era begins with the Provincial Industrial Exhibition held in Montreal, 17 to 19 October 1850, envisioned by its organizers as a rehearsal for Lower Canada's successful participation in the Great Exhibition in London the following year. Specimens of what the province had to offer in agriculture, commerce, art, technology, and industry were assembled, and a selection of the best was made for exhibition in London. Participation in and reaction to the exhibition were enthusiastic. It was generally recognized as a splendid opportunity to promote Canadian industry and resources internationally with a view to increasing trade and immigration. Such hopes were not unrewarded. However, the chief gain was in a newly perceived awareness by Canadians of their potential to supply more of the needs of their own home markets. Above all, the endeavour sparked a patriotic fervour quite new to the fledgling nation-colony.

This spirit was also found elsewhere in Canada. Toronto had a like exhibition that same year, and Saint John, New Brunswick, the following year. In fact the Upper Canada Provincial Exhibitions, held in Toronto, are the forerunners of all similar exhibitions in Canada, as they were held annually from 1846. However, their impact on the design and production of silver would not seem to be as profound as that of the Lower Canada exhibitions, and even there, silver exhibits were quite sporadic. The more relevant Montreal exhibitions are those of 1850, 1853, 1858, and 1863.

The effect of these Montreal exhibitions was not immediate. Theirs was a successive reinforcement that climaxed in the exhibition of 1863. Their chief benefit in the 1850s lay in the awakening of prospective opportunities, thereby affording encouragement to silversmiths to improve their skills and to dare to challenge ever-dominant foreign competitors.

In the Montreal exhibition of 1850, the prizewinners for goldsmith's work – that is, jewellery – were George Savage & Son, and David Smillie, both of Montreal. For silversmith's work the winners were again George Savage & Son, along with Sasseville & Lespérance (François Sasseville and Pierre Lespérance) of Quebec City.[1] The *Montreal Gazette* reported on 29 October 1850 (p. 2): "We particularly admired a case of plate, consisting of various articles for tea and dinner service, all executed in Montreal, by G. Savage & Son. The style and finish of the articles were sufficient to show, that (as in many other things), there is no occasion for sending out of Canada for anything intended for table use...."

François Sasseville won his prize at the exhibition for a chalice that was described by a contemporary newspaper as

a superb piece of work graced with a beautiful finish.... the chasing on the collar does the artist great credit, for the bunches of grapes, the vine leaves, the stalks of wheat and the other fruits of the earth are all perfectly reproduced. Similar chasing ornaments the sumptuous base, a perfect complement to the cup. Both parts are adorned with beautiful medallions depicting various scenes of the Passion.[2]

According to the same writer, the real merit of Sasseville's work rests in the fact that it was wrought, whereas ecclesiastical plate imported from Europe was largely the product of mechanical methods. "The difference between the cast vessel and the chased vessel, in price and artistic merit, is akin to that which exists between a carved statue and a cast statue – one is the fruit of the artist's labours and talent, whereas the other is simply a mass formed with a single action of a shaping device." In the main, Sasseville crafted his works according to traditional methods.

Lower Canadian silversmiths participating in the Great Exhibition in London in 1851 were G. Savage & Son and Henry Laggatt of Montreal. Upper Canada had no representation. Laggatt displayed jewellery, Savage "a silver embossed tea-kettle, and engraved spectacle case. Dessert and tea spoons. Silver tablespoon and fork."[3]

Unfortunately, none of the silver shown at the 1850 and 1851 exhibitions is known other than from the above references. There is a presentation service in the Birks Collection that is associated, albeit indirectly, with the Montreal exhibition of 1850, and it fully exemplifies the first throes of a new spirit. It is a tea and coffee service (Fig. 20), struck with the mark SAVAGE in a rectangle for the retailer Savage & Lyman and made by Bohle & Hendery of Montreal. It was presented to John Leeming, a Montreal auctioneer, as a testimony of gratitude for having served as Secretary of the Executive Committee of the 1850 exhibition. The presentation did not actually take place until 30 July 1851.[4] The inscription on the coffee pot reads: *Presented / by a number of the Citizens / of MONTREAL to / John Leeming Esq.* / *in testimony of his able, zealous, / and indefatigable exertions / as SECRETARY of / the Provincial Industrial Exhibition, / held in Montreal Oct.* 1850. / *in connection with the London / exposition of the Arts of / all Nations of / 1851.*

Among Canadian silver pieces of the time, this service reveals an explicit novelty in its ornamentation of naturalistic leafage. Four sprays of maple leaves, each with a vine-like branch, creep upward from the underside of each vessel and loosely overlay and partially encase the sides of the melon-form bodies (Fig. 21). Likewise, each rim has a wreath of maple leaves. Overall, the leafage has been judiciously incorporated with both plain and engraved surfaces. The result is

a predominating quality of reserve, which is somewhat antithetical to the prevailing Victorian aesthetic with its advocacy of overall ornamentation. Canadian silver often lacks the English Victorian predisposition for extravagance and grandeur of scale, and most products are essentially modest in conception. But it is this reserve that distinguishes so much of Canadian silver of this period and gives it its peculiar appeal.

Aside from maple leaves, the naturalistic ornament of the Leeming service is seen in the oak leaf and acorn frieze on the foot of each vessel, and in the acanthus clusters at the lower part of the spouts of the tea and coffee pots. The squirrel finials are also worth mention. This tea service represents one of the first instances in which Naturalism is encountered in Canadian silver. Essentially an English style, Naturalism is inspired by Romantic attitudes toward nature. Its vigour is conspicuous in English literature and art – in landscape painting, for example, and in the predilection of the English for horticulture and landscape gardening. As a style in silver, Naturalism is an outgrowth of the Rococo Revival, with which it coexists throughout the 1840s, 50s, and 60s. Its popularity in England peaks in the early 1850s, and it is about this time that it was adopted in Canada. It should be added that in Canadian silver this style finds expression in ornamentation rather than in the forms of objects. This is true for the Leeming service. In general, elements from the Rococo Revival and Naturalism are mingled in varying amounts.

An important component of Naturalism is appropriateness of ornament. Indeed it was a Victorian maxim that ornament was to be in sympathy with the function of an object. The ornament on the Leeming tea service is not superfluous; on the contrary, it has a definite emblematic character. As early as 1805 the maple leaf was regarded by French Canadians as their particular emblem; by 1850 it had also gained acceptance in English-speaking parts of the country. For the several decades that follow, it is one of the most common decorative motifs on Canadian silver. Contemporaneously, the maple leaf also appears on English pottery made for the Canadian market, and afterwards Canadian-made pottery. The deliberate evocation of patriotism in the Leeming service is in keeping with the spirit of the Montreal exhibition that it celebrates.

23

20

The oak leaves also have a relevance: they allude to England and indirectly to the impending Great Exhibition.[5]

The nationalist theme is continued in the Great Seal of the Province of Canada (Canada East and Canada West, later Quebec and Ontario) engraved prominently on the tea and coffee pots (Fig. 22).[6] Here the seal is flanked on the left by ships' masts (at a wharf?) and a steam engine, on the right by a beehive and ploughshare, signifying commerce, industry, and agriculture, which were being promoted by the exhibition. The coat-of-arms of the city of Montreal is engraved on the two smaller vessels, and on all four is a palm tree, the Leeming (or more correctly Fleming or Fleeming) crest.

Not just in matters of style, ornament, and expression of patriotic character, but also from the technical standpoint, the Leeming service is a fine example of Canadian innovative work. Handles, spouts, finials, feet and the applied maple leaves are all cast. Such extensive casting by a silversmith was unprecedented in Canada. Bohle & Hendery were willing experimenters in this period when silver-making worldwide was undergoing dramatic technological changes.

Public reaction to the Leeming service was most favourable, if it is to be gauged from the *Montreal Gazette*: "The workmanship is very fine, worthy a place in the [Great] Exhibition itself."[7] Whereas Peter Bohle and Robert Hendery are the silversmiths, the above article informs us that James Duncan (1806–1881) was responsible for the design, and George Matthews (active c.1842–1864) for the engraving. As little is known about the designing of early Canadian silver, the fact of Duncan's involvement is of special interest. Other than for exceptional commissions, silversmiths up to this time probably drafted their own designs. Were they now relying more on artist-designers, as was certainly the case in the decade that follows?

James Duncan was one of the few professional artists in Montreal at mid-century. He is best known for his watercolours of landscapes, and street and genre scenes, mainly of Montreal and vicinity. He also painted landscapes in oil, and portraits and miniatures, among other things. Another instance of his collaboration with Matthews was in a series of six views of Montreal, for

21

22

20 Tea and coffee service, designed by James Duncan, engraved by George Matthews. Maker's mark of Bohle & Hendery for Savage & Lyman, 1851. Silver, cream jug and sugar bowl gilt lined; 29 cm high (coffee pot). Birks (24122–24125).

21 Teapot in Fig. 20. Maker's mark of Bohle & Hendery for Savage & Lyman, 1851. Silver, ivory insulators; 24.5 cm high. Birks (24122).

22 Great Seal of the Province of Canada. Detail of coffee pot in Fig. 20. Birks (24125).

which Duncan was the designer and Matthews the lithographer. These were published in 1843–44. Whether or not Duncan did other silver designs remains uncertain. But we do know that he executed designs for a "provincial coinage," which were exhibited at the Montreal and London exhibitions of 1850 and 1851.[8]

Unfortunately, innovative forays such as that demonstrated in the Leeming service, however modest, are rare until the end of the decade, despite the fact that presentation silver was increasing in popularity in Canada. For all its deliberate if not over-conscious "Canadianism," the Leeming service betrays the era's reliance on imported silverware, as the tray (Fig. 23) that originally accompanied it was made in Sheffield, England.

Imports dominate the decade, and pieces of a grand, as well as modest nature are found among them. Of the imported trophies, a fine specimen is the Jubilee Trophy of the (Royal) Montreal Curling Club (Fig. 24), which is blazoned with the Scotch thistle. This pitcher was purchased by voluntary subscription in celebration of the club's fiftieth anniversary in 1857.[9] The Montreal club is the oldest one of its kind in North America. Curling was of course originally a Scottish sport, and the Montreal Curling Club, long after its founding, vigorously maintained this national character. Membership was almost exclusive to Scots by birth or descent. Even this trophy was ordered from Scotland, and it has an unidentified mark MACKAY in a rounded rectangle, and Edinburgh hallmarks for 1856–57.[10]

Most presentation silver imported into Canada in the second half of the nineteenth century was made in England. An impressive example is a silver fountain presented to Sir William Logan in March 1859. Logan, the founder and first director of the Geological Survey of Canada, and in effect the father of Canadian geology, did much to promote Canadian mineral resources internationally. His reputation was far-reaching: he was elected a fellow of the Royal Society in 1851, awarded the Cross of the Legion of Honour by the Emperor of France, Napoleon III, in 1855, and knighted by Queen Victoria in 1856. Wishing to pay tribute to an illustrious native son, a number of citizens of Montreal presented Logan with a "massive" silver fountain made by R. & S. Garrard & Co. of London. From descriptions we know that this fountain consisted of several basins, one above the other, and was mounted on a pedestal of ebony representing a bed of coal. The whole incorporated engraved illustrations of the palaeontology of the Carboniferous era. The reference is to Logan's concept of the origin of coal, one of his great contributions to the science of geology.[11]

Another later example fashioned by R. & S. Garrard and Co. of London is a large service of plate (Fig. 25) given as a testimonial to Edwin H. King on his retirement as president of the Bank of Montreal in June 1873. The service cost the shareholders of the bank some $10 000.[12] In addition to Garrard & Co., names of English manufacturers most often encountered are: Hunt & Roskell, Edward Barnard & Sons, and Hawksworth, Eyre & Co. with Joseph Walker (& Co.) as agent in Montreal, Elkington & Co., and William Hutton & Sons with James Hutton (& Co.) as agent in Montreal. The last three supplied electroplate (silverplate) as well as silver. A smaller number of American suppliers were located chiefly in New York State.

The only considerable and sustained competition that imports were to know from a Canadian maker for the remainder of the nineteenth century comes from Robert Hendery and the Hendery firms, starting about 1858–59. Not limiting his efforts to domestic and presentation silver, Hendery also gains a good portion of the church market, both Roman Catholic and Protestant. He first wins control of the Montreal market, the major metropolitan centre in Canada, and during the early 1860s gradually infiltrates the national market. By the late 1870s, Hendery is supplying dealers from coast to coast.

An early hint of the rising Canadian challenge to imports is evidenced at the Montreal Provincial Exhibition of 1858 when a journalist writes about Robert Hendery, "This exhibitor showed a marked improvement over previous years."[13] Hendery in fact won prizes for the best displays of silver and electroplate.[14] However, a summary description of his display does indicate that it was still relatively modest, "Comprising samples of medals, cups, also a fine fish knife and fork."[15] The decisiveness of the challenge becomes apparent in subsequent years when Hendery greatly increases his output of presentation plate.

23

24

25 Service of presentation plate, manufactured by R. & S. Garrard & Co. of London, England. A wood engraving in the *Canadian Illustrated News,* Montreal, 14 June 1873, p. 373.

25

The factors governing this increased production are no doubt numerous. A rapidly increasing population could only mean an expanding market for local industry, regardless of an increase in the number of imports. A buoyant economy was another factor contributing to this upturn. And, as stated earlier, the new custom of provincial exhibitions may have induced a more favourable climate, at least in Montreal.

Internal factors are also at work. Within the craft there were dramatic changes in production methods. Increasing mechanization on the one hand, and the gradual disappearance of small independent workshops on the other, favoured consolidation into fewer and fewer large operations – a process that began much earlier in Britain and the United States. Granted, the scale of production in the Canadian industry was relatively modest. Even the operations of larger Canadian silversmiths – Hendery, for example – were quite small by American or British standards. Nevertheless, the Canadians' receptiveness to innovation led to a greater efficiency and economy of production, with a corresponding increase in their competitive status.

All else aside, the crux of the issue of augmented silver production at the end of the 1850s may well rest with the availability of the raw material. Native silver was not mined in Canada in any quantity before 1869. This paucity of metal impeded the full prospering of silversmithing in Canada and accounted in part for the plenitude of imports.

The early history of silver mining in Canada is very sketchy. Silver deposits were known to exist on the north shore of Lake Superior as early as the late eighteenth century.[16] Interest in these deposits was not rekindled until 1846, and it is not certain whether there was even then any concerted attempt at exploitation. Incentive was no doubt frustrated by government regulations, as all rights to gold and silver discoveries were reserved for the Crown.[17] This could mean that some mining was being done surreptitiously, which would explain the scarcity of accounts on the subject. Nonetheless, by 1848 the British North American Mining Company was shipping silver to Montreal.[18]

Among others, Sir William Logan did much to promote awareness of these deposits, and samples of Lake Superior silver were part of the outstanding displays of Canadian minerals at the Great Exhibition in London of 1851 and the Universal Exhibition in Paris of 1855.[19] However, one of the first mentions of an object actually being fashioned from Canadian silver is in conjunction with the above-mentioned Hendery displays at the Provincial Exhibition of 1858: "These specimens were manufactured from native silver obtained from Lake Superior...."[20] Such references are quite frequent from then on and invariably mention Lake Superior when the source of the metal is specified.

The inescapable conclusion is that Canadian mines were supplying much-needed silver metal by the end of the 1850s. Even though the quantities could not have been great, the fact is not without significance, as previously there had been absolutely no local source for the metal. By 1867 the government revoked its restrictions on silver mining, which resulted in increased exploration. In 1869 the well-known Silver Islet mine went into operation and continued as an abundant producer until 1884. Other small discoveries were made in Quebec and Nova Scotia. However, the real bonanza occurred at Cobalt in 1904.[21]

Clearly this new supply of metal played a role in vitalizing the silver-making industry in Canada. Hendery no doubt benefited especially. His success is also due, in large part, to his astuteness in correctly assessing public tastes, and in daring to compete with imports. Production of presentation silver in Canada is at its height in this half century, with Hendery as the chief maker.

Notes

1. *Montreal Gazette*, 24 Oct. 1850, p. 2.
2. *Journal de Québec*, 17 Oct. 1850, p. 2 [Trans.]. Also G. Morisset, "L'orfèvre François Sasseville," *Mémoires de la Société Royale du Canada*, 3rd ser., XLIX, sect. 1 (1955), p. 52.
3. *Great Exhibition of the Works of Industry of All Nations, 1851. Official Descriptive and Illustrated Catalogue* (London: Spicer Brothers, 1851), Vol. II, p. 968. Also *Canada at the Universal Exhibition of 1855* (Toronto: John Lovell, 1856), p. 23.
4. *Montreal Gazette*, 28 July 1851, p. 2; *Montreal Transcript*, 2 Aug. 1851, p. 2; *Morning Chronicle* [Quebec], 30 July 1851, p. 2.
5. *Morning Chronicle* [Quebec], 30 July 1851, p. 2.
6. C. Swan, *Canada: Symbols of Sovereignty* (Toronto: University of Toronto Press, 1977), pp. 168–169.
7. 28 July 1851, p. 2.

8. *Montreal Gazette*, 24 Oct. 1850, p. 2; "List of Articles For-warded from Montreal for the Grand Exhibition in London...," 1 Mar. 1851. McGill University, McLennan Library, Depart-ment of Rare Books and Special Collections, Lyman Family, Miscellaneous Papers. Duncan is also sometimes said to have designed the "Habitant" penny and halfpenny tokens for the Bank of Montreal, the City Bank, the Banque du Peuple, and the Quebec Bank, in 1837; and the Bank of Montreal tokens of like denominations, with "front view of the bank" and "front and side views," in 1837 and 1838 respectively. J.R. Harper, *Early Painters and Engravers in Canada* (Toronto: University of Toronto Press, 1970), pp. 97–98; P.A. Todd, *James D. Duncan (1806–1881): Catalogue of Works and Introduction to His Art*, M.A. Thesis (Concordia University, 1978), p. 208; P. Montgomery, *The Romance of Canada's Money* (Toronto: The Macmillan Company of Canada Limited, 1973), pp. 22–23.

9. *One Hundred and Fifty Years of Curling 1807–1957: The Royal Montreal Curling Club* (Montreal: Privately Printed, 1957), p. 27.

10. Scottish marks of this period have not been properly studied. This mark may belong to John Mackay of Mackay & Chisholm or to James Mackay of Mackay, Cunningham & Co.; letter of Elizabeth Wright, 29 Aug. 1983.

11. *Montreal Transcript*, 19 Mar. 1859, p. 2; C.G. Winder, "Where Is Logan's Silver Fountain?" *Proceedings of the Geological Association of Canada*, XVIII (1967), pp. 115–118; B.J. Harrington, *Life of Sir William E. Logan, Kt.* (Montreal: Dawson Brothers, 1883), pp. 319–320.

12. *Canadian Illustrated News* [Montreal], 14 June 1873, pp. 371, 373.

13. *Montreal Gazette*, 7 Oct. 1858, p. 2.

14. *Montreal Gazette*, 1 Oct. 1858, p. 1.

15. *Montreal Gazette*, 7 Oct. 1858, p. 2.

16. "Shores of Lake Superior," *Canadian Illustrated News* [Hamilton], 13 June 1863, p. 53.

17. B.H. Scott, "The Story of Silver Islet," *Ontario History*, XLIX (1957), p. 125.

18. *Morning Courier* [Montreal], 10 Feb. 1848, p. 2.

19. *Great Exhibition Official Catalogue*, pp. 959–961; *Canada at the Universal Exhibition of 1855*, p. 18; W.E. Logan and T.S. Hunt, *A Sketch of the Geology of Canada Serving to Explain the Geological Map and the Collection of Economic Minerals Sent to the Universal Exhibition at Paris, 1855* (Paris: Hector Bossange & Sons, 1855), pp. 423, 450.

20. *Montreal Gazette*, 1 Oct. 1858, p. 1.

21. T.A. Rickard, "The Silver Islet," *Canadian Mining Journal*, LXIII (1942), pp. 565–569; B. White, *Silver, Its History and Romance* (London: Hodder and Stoughton, 1917), pp. 61–68.

Chapter III

1850–1899: Makers and Retailers

In the second half of the nineteenth century, the numbers of traditional silversmiths continue to diminish in favour of the manufacturing silversmith. This is striking in light of the phenomenal growth in Canada's population and a corresponding expansion of the market for silver. On the other hand, retail silversmiths – who for the most part are jewellers in the modern sense – proliferate and establish the support network essential for marketing. Between "maker" and "retailer" there is a somewhat nebulous sector, that of the combined maker and retailer. This third sector continues to reflect to some extent the original craft organization of independent silversmiths.

Individuals belonging to any particular one of these sectors are not always readily identified. For the most part, this is because of the absence in Canada during the nineteenth century of an official state-regulated system ensuring the mandatory and consistent marking of silver wares. Advertisements, newspaper notices, directories and other records employ a nomenclature that is often deliberately ambiguous, offering little to clarify the status of a so-called silversmith. Retailers are frequently referred to as silversmiths or manufacturing silversmiths when in fact they only commission works and thus function as intermediaries between maker and customer. There is some overlapping of the sectors, and no standard pattern emerges of internal organization governing the various aspects of manufacture and marketing, both wholesale and retail.

Some manufacturers sell their wares, retail as well as wholesale; in other words they can be classified as manufacturing retailers. Furthermore, a manufacturing retailer might sell only his own wares, or those of others in addition to his own. Likewise, a retail silversmith might be a simple retailer, or both wholesaler and retailer. Many independent silversmiths prefer to retail their own wares exclusively. On the other hand, there are "makers to the trade," both in the form of large workshop (or factory) operations, and individual "outworkers" who work exclusively for other makers or retailers. The products of these operations often go unrecorded as the makers are not always inclined to mark them. Compounding the overall problem is the fact that identity marks on a piece of silver may represent a maker or a retailer or both (see Appendix I).

This confusion has its roots in Canada in the late eighteenth century. It becomes more acute in the early nineteenth century, with the transition from the traditional to the modern organization of the industry, and persists well into the later part of the century. Thus it is not always possible to identify the maker of a piece of Canadian silver from this period. Nor is the situation exclusive to Canada, although it does have its national peculiarities. The same general situation exists in the United States, where there was a much greater impetus for centralization of the industry, and to a degree also in Britain.

While a few firms dominate in various regions of Canada, two are in the forefront nationally. Both are Montreal-based. Robert Hendery, as previously stated, is the single most important manufacturer. His retailing counterparts are the various Savage firms. Not unexpectedly, there is an interaction and an element of interdependence between the two, at least for a period. In the realm of presentation silver, Hendery was the leading maker, while the Savage firms had a comparable though not equivalent role as retailer.

George Savage Sr (1767–1845) is the progenitor of the Savage firms. An accomplished watchmaker, he first practised his craft in his native town of Huddersfield, Yorkshire, England. He also worked in London for a few years before emigrating to Montreal in 1818. During his first year in Canada he entered into a short-lived partnership with James Adams Dwight. By 1819 he was on his own. It seems that from the outset Savage was simply a retailer, notwithstanding his earlier contributions to watchmaking: in 1818, for example, he had patented a remontoir; in 1822 he received an award from the Society of Arts (London) for his somewhat earlier invention of a lever escapement for watches known as the "Savage two pin." Sometime before

1828, George Savage took his son Joseph into partnership, as George Savage & Son. The father retired about 1836, and by 1842 the business was completely transferred to Joseph.[1] George Savage Sr died 21 July 1845; nevertheless, the name George Savage & Son was retained by the business until the end of the decade.

At one time the Savages had two stores in Montreal and another in Toronto. The principal Montreal store knew several locations, eventually settling at the corner of Notre Dame and St Gabriel Streets in 1838. The other store was at 123 St Paul Street, with William Learmont as manager for a period until 1841; it closed the following year. John Wood managed the Notre Dame Street store for several years until 1839. Both Wood and Learmont were well-known Montreal watchmakers and jewellers. The Toronto store opened in 1829, with George Savage Jr in charge. By 1843 that store was taken over by George Jr, and the name and any ties to George Savage & Son were relinquished.

The firm of George Savage & Son usually advertised as "manufacturers & importers of watches, clocks, jewellery & silver ware, wholesale and retail,"[2] although we know they were principally retailers. A great deal of the Savages' stock was imported from Britain, where Joseph Savage did much of the buying. Most of the silver they sold was also imported, and only a small percentage was obtained locally. Very little if any silver was actually made in the Savage workshop. At the time it was customary for retailers to take full credit as makers of their products. For example, the later firm of Savage & Lyman invariably calls itself the manufacturer of all silver in its displays at the provincial exhibitions, when that was certainly not the case.

It is highly improbable that either George Sr or Joseph Savage made silver themselves. Whether one or more silversmiths were active in their workshop has yet to be clarified. Savage did advertise in *La Minerve* [Quebec], 15 August 1836 (p. 4): "Horloges, montres, ouvrages en argent et bijouterie réparés avec soin et promptitude." There may at least have been someone in their workshop who dealt with repairs and smallwork. In any event, Savage must have had some kind of contractual arrangement with various local silversmiths to ensure a regular supply of silver wares. The nature of these agreements can only be conjectured. A study of marks (pseudo-hallmarks) reveals that at

some point Savage was supplied by Salomon Marion and Nelson Walker, among others. Pertinent also is P.W. Wood's recollection in a letter to Henry Birks in 1904: "When Lord Durham was Governor General, he offered a prize for something – a silver cup to cost £100. Mr. Savage accepted the order, and it was made in a little silversmiths shop on a lane off Jacques Cartier Square and near St. Vincent Street."[3] That silversmith can be none other than Paul Morand (1784–1854). The cup referred to is probably the Governor-General's Cup for horse racing which, according to the *Montreal Gazette* of 21 August 1838 (p. 2), was competed for in Montreal that day. Tradition also holds (and this is more or less substantiated by a study of marks) that Savage had a long-standing agreement with Peter Bohle (1786–1862), who produced mainly flatware, and, by the late 1830s, also with Robert Hendery (see below).

That Savage dealt in considerable quantities of silver is confirmed by an advertisement in the *Montreal Gazette* of 28 June 1848 (p. 3), in which the firm claims to have on hand "3,000 oz of silver plate, both imported and of their own manufacture, consisting in part of – tea and coffee sets, trays, cake baskets, goblets, cups, etc." It also seems that the earlier severance of ties with George Savage Jr in Toronto did not lead to a reduced interest in the Upper Canadian market. On 22 September 1849, Savage advertises again in the *Montreal Gazette* (p. 3) that they are "prepared to offer a liberal discount to the trade and Upper Canada merchants, on wholesale purchases."

Savage enters a new phase in 1851 when Theodore Lyman joins his brother-in-law Joseph Savage as a partner in the business, now named Savage & Lyman. Lyman was born in Northampton, Massachusetts, in 1818, and moved with his family to Montreal in 1833. His sister, Abigail Jones Lyman, had married Joseph Savage in 1829. The Savage & Lyman store was relocated to the Cathedral Block on Notre Dame Street (No. 159½; after 1864 No. 271) in 1858. Joseph Savage died the following year, on 6 February, at the age of sixty.

In 1868 Lyman took two others into partnership: Charles W. Hagar, the office manager, and Henry Birks, the store manager. The firm became Savage, Lyman & Co. George Berger was also in charge of the Savage

Chapter III

jewellery factory about this time. In 1872 the store was again moved, to 226 and 228 St James Street. Because of the depression of the 1870s, the firm soon experienced financial difficulties. Birks withdrew from the partnership in 1877, and the following year the firm failed and went into liquidation. It is not surprising to learn that most of the creditors were British.[4] The business was restarted by December 1878 and took on the old name Savage & Lyman.[5] It never regained its former stature, however, and lasted only until 1885.

The Savage firm was the largest and most prestigious retail jeweller and silversmith in Canada in the second quarter of the nineteenth century. Its business sphere extended beyond its provincial borders into Upper Canada. Of all firms, whether manufacturer or retailer, it was the most regular exhibitor at the various provincial exhibitions, winning many prizes over the years, and not only in Lower Canada. For example, at the Provincial Exhibition in Kingston in 1859, it won first prize. According to a contemporary account, the Savage display consisted of a silver tea and coffee service; trays, claret jugs, cups and goblets; forks, spoons, ladles; a plate chest complete with forks, spoons, and knives; and a fish knife and fork. Public reaction was most favourable: "The whole reflected the greatest credit on the exhibitors and on Canadian workmanship; and proved that greater perfection is reached in this kind of work in Canada than many people are apt to imagine."[6]

Hendery was the major Canadian maker of silver for the Savage firms during this period. There were others, but most fall into the category of unidentified "makers to the trade." Among them were Bohle & Denman, a partnership of George David Bohle (1831–1869) and William Henry Denman (active c.1859–1900), from about 1864 until 1867. Bohle & Denman were flatware specialists.[7]

Robert Hendery founded the Hendery firms. The story of his early life and career have yet to be recounted. He was born on the island of Corfu, Greece, about 1814, presumably of Scottish parents – at least his father was Scottish. It has long been held that he emigrated from Scotland to Montreal sometime in the late 1830s, at the instigation of George Savage, and was employed by George Savage & Son. By 1840 he was on his own. In the years following he probably had

some kind of working association with Peter Bohle, and also with Francis (also Charles-François) Bohle (1822–1860), the son of Peter. One of the few early records concerning Hendery gives the date of his marriage to Sarah (Mary) Maysenhoelder (also Maysenholder) as 16 May 1843. He was a widower, and Sarah was the daughter of the Montreal silversmith John Maysenhoelder. Both Maysenhoelder and his wife Margaret were sponsors at the baptisms of children of Peter Bohle between 1821 and 1823. Francis Bohle was a witness to the second marriage of Robert Hendery, as well as sponsor at the baptism of Hendery's daughter Eliza in 1848. The social and personal ties between the Bohles, Maysenhoelders, and Henderys were ostensibly very close.

As "makers to the trade," Peter Bohle and Robert Hendery were the major suppliers of Savage and of others. Eventually they entered into a full-fledged partnership, as Bohle & Hendery, by 1851 at the latest. That partnership was terminated about 1856. Most of their activity was relatively covert, for they advertised little, did not exhibit, and received almost no public recognition. An exception is their submission of "specimens of electroplating on brass" to the Provincial Exhibition at Montreal in 1855. The same pieces were sent to the Universal Exhibition at Paris that year.[8] Bohle & Hendery were among the first electroplaters in Canada.

With his independence from Bohle, Hendery's business entered a flourishing new phase. Coincidentally, he began to exhibit publicly in his own name on a fairly regular basis, and now received proper credit for at least some of his work. He also turned to the retail as well as the wholesale market, although he continued for some time to sell from his factory. As noted in the preceding chapter, his production of hollow ware and presentation pieces grew considerably from this time onward. So did acclaim.

In *Mackay's Montreal Directory, 1857–8* (p. 410), Hendery advertises as a "Silversmith and Jeweller, Plater, &c... Manufacturer of tea sets, cups, trays, pitchers, spoons, forks, fish and butter knives, military ornaments. Electro-silvering and gilding in all its branches; house and carriage plating, and jobbing in jewellery and silverware promptly attended to." The Hendery factory relocated a number of times. By 1856

34

it was at 154 Craig Street, by 1862 at 112 Craig, by 1865 at 590 Craig, by 1869 at 108 St Peter Street, by 1872 at 184 St Peter, and by 1880 at 134 St Peter where it remained until 1899. Hendery also opened a store by early 1866 at 53 Great St James Street. It moved to 157 St James Street in 1870 and closed by 1871. This is the only time that Hendery is recorded as having a retail store. It was during the period when he had both a factory and a store that the firm became known as Robert Hendery & Co.; thereafter it reverted to the old designation consisting of the owner's name only: Robert Hendery. From about 1870 he was solely a manufacturing silversmith.

John Leslie (1849–1939) was apprenticed to Hendery on 5 November 1864, and Albert Dumouchel (1860–1940) was apprenticed on 5 November 1874. Otherwise, little is known of those who worked for the Hendery firm at this time and even less is known about the firm's general organization. The census of 1861 indicates that Hendery was employing six persons that year. Fortunately, a document does survive (see Appendix II) which describes the factory as it existed in 1894.

In 1887 Hendery took John Leslie into partnership and the name of the firm became Hendery & Leslie. Hendery retired in 1895 and ownership devolved to Leslie. In 1897 Hendery died. In 1899 the firm was absorbed by Henry Birks & Sons, and Leslie stayed on as manager of the Birks silver factory until his retirement in 1925.[9]

These, then, are the Hendery firms that dominate the sphere of Canadian presentation silver. Hendery's production of this kind of ware started to escalate at the end of the 1850s, but it is really at the Provincial Exhibition of 1863 at Montreal that the full extent and high quality of these works was recognized. There Hendery won first prize in his category, and the quantity of silver he exhibited was sizable.[10] He was acclaimed a master silversmith, equal to any, particularly to the makers of the imported wares. The Hendery reputation for presentation silver was fixed for several decades to come.

The *Montreal Gazette*, 17 September 1863 (p. 2), gives a full account of this display:

> Mr. Hendery, Silversmith, Craig Street, shows a very fine collection of "Presentation Plate," con-

sisting of tea and coffee sets, cups, goblets, epergnes, &c., all of solid silver. For beauty of design, mechanical skill, and perfectness of finish, this collection would rank with the finest specimens of silver work from any establishment in the world.

Among the items was a

> Tea and coffee set intended for presentation by the Richelieu Navigation Company to Mr. [J.F.] Sincennes. On one part of the body of the tea and coffee pot, is a pretty view of the Town of Sorel, with the Steamer *Montreal* entering that harbor; above is a shield bearing Mr. Sincennes' crest; the top of the lid combining a group of marine emblems, underneath which is a wreath of water lilies. On another part of the body is a beautiful model bust of the recipient. A splendid figure of Jacques Cartier is presented on a third portion of the body, while a majestic Prince of Wales Plume ornaments the fourth. The cost of this presentation set will be over $1,300.

Among the trophies were "the 'Corinthian' Race Cup, won by Major Penn's favorite horse 'Gunner' a short time since. Also, the 'Montreal Hunt Cup,' won by Capt. DeWinton's celebrated horse 'Tearaway'." There was also a variety of goblets "prominent among which is the one recently presented to Mr. Bertram, by the Fire Brigade, and another presented to Mr. Cooper by the members of the Fire Department." The goblet given to Captain Peter Cooper by the members of the Protector Fire Company, No. 4, had a fitting design:

> The base represents the top of a hydrant, on which three cross hose keys encircled with a wreath of laurels are placed, the cup resting on the wrench part of the keys, on two sides of which are traced the rose shamrock and thistle, on one side is a representation of a horse reel and fireman in full uniform.[11]

The pièce de résistance of the Hendery display was a centrepiece that had been commissioned for presentation to the Honourable George-Étienne Cartier by his constituents. Unfortunately, no image of this work is known to exist, and we must rely again on the *Montreal Gazette* account:

The base of this testimonial is of triangular shape, richly ornamented with scrolls, and having a shield on either side, one of which bears a modelled likeness of the honored recipient; another the inscription; the third a beautiful likeness of our beloved Sovereign, Queen Victoria, in her Royal robes, and holding the sceptre of authority in her hand. These shields are encircled by wreaths of the maple leaf, springing from a union cluster of the rose, thistle, and shamrock. Over the base is a group of three figures – Jacques Cartier, representing the first of navigators; Montcalm, the first of French Generals; Bishop Plessis, the first Church representative in Canada. From the centre of this group rises a Maple Tree – emblem of Canada – from the trunk of which, spring six branches in rich foliage. These branches may be adapted to holding lights or jellies. The trunk is capped by a large Crystal Fruit Basket. The cost of this testimonial will be about $2,500.

This description calls to mind such grand imported works as the centrepiece by Edward Barnard & Sons presented to William Morris (Fig. 19). It testifies to an extraordinary piece of workmanship for a Canadian silversmith. It also demonstrates Hendery's resolve to challenge foreign – particularly English – competitors on all levels. Most of his presentation plate is composed of rather ordinary works for general consumption. But among the remainder is a group conceived as elegant and monumental creations which might be loosely dubbed "art silver." Hendery stands alone among early Canadian silversmiths for this type of production. Generally, these works assume the form of centrepieces (epergnes) and candelabra, and even silver sculpture. Sometimes all these aspects are incorporated in a single work, as in the Cartier centrepiece which also has a group of statuettes. The purpose of these pieces was display, and consequently they sometimes border on the extravagant in their embellishments. They are the showiest and most elaborate items of plate made in Canada during the Victorian period, and they represent Hendery's major contribution to Canadian silver.

In June 1863 an art critic for *Les Beaux-Arts* (I, 3, p. 22) gave his enthusiastic approval of Hendery's newly demonstrated achievement in this area: "We were not mistaken concerning Mr. Hendery's talent. He is a true artist, and the items he so kindly showed us are evidence that Montreal currently has some remarkable men in its midst, men who will inspire progress in the arts." He goes on to assert that the Cartier centrepiece denotes "Mr. Hendery's desire to rank with the best silversmiths in the city." These words represent a fair summation of Hendery's stature at the time – not only in Montreal but also in Canada as a whole.

The *Montreal Gazette* concludes its description of Hendery's display at the 1863 exhibition thus: "Altogether these specimens of workmanship and mechanical skill are creditable in the highest degree to Mr. Hendery's establishment, affording the most convincing proof that Canada need not in future import presentation sets from abroad." Similar sentiments would be voiced about Hendery in a number of newspaper articles over the years to come.

Hendery owed his success in no small degree to his designers. The design for the Cartier centrepiece was drawn up by Louis Fréret (Frerêt ?). *Les Beaux-Arts* (I, 3, p. 22) gives notice that Fréret's talent "is confirmed by his more than twenty years of experience with the best silversmiths in the metropolis of London." This statement would suggest that this Louis Fréret is the same person as the French artist-designer who was engaged by the London manufacturing silversmiths Edward Barnard & Sons and C.F. Hancock. He furnished designs for silver sculpture, including Hancock's well-known "Robin Hood contending for the Golden Arrow," the Goodwood Cup of 1850, which was exhibited at the Great Exhibition.[12] To give some measure of the calibre of Fréret, it need only be added that Hancock, along with Garrard and Hunt & Roskell, was the leading maker in England of silver sculpture.

Thus Hendery was not simply imitating his English rivals but was trying to equal them by employing one of their own designers. More than anything else, this access to skilled designers helped place Hendery on a firm competitive footing. Also somewhat curious is the fact that Fréret was a Frenchman. At this period it was fashionable among English manufacturing silversmiths to rely on foreign, largely French, designers. Hendery obviously shared this preference.

Why Fréret came to Canada is uncertain, and his activity here is somewhat of a mystery. Montreal city directories do indicate that he was living in that city during the years 1863–1865, 1871–1872, and 1878. His profession is given as either sculptor or moulder. The Canada Census for 1871 enumerates him as an artist, born in France, and sixty-five years of age. He did exhibit a statuette entitled "Knight in Armour – time, Reign of Henry the Fifth" at the first exhibition of the Society of Canadian Artists in Montreal in 1868, and three others entitled "Duck Shooting" at the seventh exhibition of the Montreal Art Association in 1872. In addition, a statuette, "The Canadian Trapper," modelled by Fréret while he was working at Forsyth's Marble Works in Montreal, was engraved for the *Canadian Illustrated News* [Montreal], 4 March 1871 (pp. 130, 136). Otherwise, details of Fréret's career in Canada are not forthcoming.

Was the Cartier centrepiece the only assignment Hendery ever commissioned from Fréret? Hendery must have turned to local artists for designs from time to time. For instance, Alfred Sandham designed the silver trowel executed by Hendery for the laying of the cornerstone of the Young Men's Christian Association building in Montreal in September 1872.[13] There is also firm evidence that Hendery had his own resident artist-designer – Felix Louis Paris – as was the practice with most large English manufacturing silversmiths.

One of the earliest records of Paris's presence in Hendery's workshop is in May of 1858. It is in conjunction with a silver inkstand intended as a testimonial to the liberation of a slave by his master, the Honourable Hamnett K. Pinhey of March Township, Member of the Legislative Council of the Province of Canada (1847–1857). The piece was commissioned and designed by Pinhey's son-in-law, Dr Hamnett Hill, of Bytown, present-day Ottawa. The wafer box (for small wafer-like seals) was surmounted by the figure of a slave rendered kneeling in prayer, with his chains still lying at his side, as if at the very moment of emancipation. This inkstand was modelled by Felix Paris, and although small-scale, it would have been one of the earliest examples of silver sculpture from the Hendery workshop.[14]

Otherwise, records pertaining to Paris are somewhat sporadic. Apparently he continued to be connected with Hendery as late as 1877. He is variously credited with being an engraver, artist, designer, modeller, silversmith, silverchaser, and so on. He was no doubt all of these. Certainly it must be more than coincidence that the rather sudden rise in the quality and quantity of Hendery's wares corresponds with the time when Paris is known to have entered the workshop. In the hierarchical division of labour typical of large English manufacturing silversmiths, the artist-designers and modellers were at the top of the scale. Then followed the silverchasers, the most highly skilled of the silverworkers. The Hendery operation, being comparatively small, certainly could not have afforded such individual specialists. Therefore, the appearance of someone like the multi-talented Paris would have been an extraordinary asset. Hendery's designs become more elaborate at this time and there is a great increase in chased ornament, suggesting a trained silverchaser. Is this due to Paris as well?

We know that in the later years of Hendery & Leslie, until about 1896, John Leslie did all the designing and chasing (see Appendix II). Paris was probably the forerunner of Leslie in his capacity as designer-silverchaser, and all indications are that his role in the Hendery enterprise was a vital one. In addition to the aforementioned functions, he also managed Hendery's retail store for its duration from 1866 to 1870/71. Subsequently, in about 1871, Paris also got involved in the manufacture of electroplate. In 1872 he was in partnership with Cornelius C. Jenking, in Paris & Jenking (or Jenking & Paris), electroplaters. They were located at 637 Craig Street and 51 St Joseph. The latter site was also the home of the Dominion Nickel Plating Co., of which Hendery was superintendent in addition to his other endeavours. The Paris & Jenking firm was out of business by 1874, and Jenking continued on alone for another year. The Dominion Nickel Plating Co. also ceased operations and was succeeded by the nickel-plating works of T.L. Clark in 1874.[15]

The ties of Felix Paris to Hendery were personal as well as professional. He married Hendery's daughter Sarah on 27 June 1867 at Trinity (Anglican) Church, Montreal. The couple also had several children baptized at that same church. From the Canada Census of 1861 and 1871 it has been established that Paris was born in England, of French extraction. Presumably he was trained in England.[16] There is a discrepancy in the

37

ages given by the censuses: one gives twenty-six, the other thirty-four, which would mean Paris was born between about 1835 and 1837.

Of silver pieces that can be positively identified with Paris the most outstanding is the Stephens Testimonial (Fig. 26) by Hendery. The recipient was George Washington Stephens, and it was presented by a group of Montreal citizens in April 1877 in recognition of Stephens's ten years of service as an alderman. As a silver sculpture, it displays an intrinsic Classical aspect in the geometric disposition of its elements, in its restraint, and its monumental character. It contrasts markedly with the decorative extravagance and exuberance of so many English examples of this period. It is nevertheless indisputably Victorian in its symbolic content, which is slightly abstruse, as the *Canadian Illustrated News* of 19 May 1877 observes:

The figures most prominently represented are Justice with her sword and scales, with a very well modelled figure of a handsome dog, "The Faithful Watchdog," representing the soubriquet with which Ald. Stephens has been designated by the citizens owing to the part he has often assumed in Council on the questions that come before that body.

Reputed for his integrity and as a champion of good government and the public interest thoughout his political career, even later as a member of the Quebec Assembly (he was elected in 1881, 1892, and 1897), Stephens headed many a government investigation and was popularly known as "Watch Dog." The description continues:

The figures are supported by a pedestal sexiform and with six panels of frosted silver which rest upon the base of solid silver heavily moulded, and this in turn is supported upon the heavy ebony foundation, also sexiform and polished, and moulded handsomely. Standing on the silver base on each side of the pedestal are the figures representing trade and commerce (a sailor with coils of rope and barrels), and manufactures (a mechanic with hammer, anvil and implements of machinery). At the foot of the pedestal, where it swells to form the base or the front, is the lion

rampant and motto in scroll, *"Virtutis Amore,"* and on the reverse side the monogram "G.W.S.," while on the other four spaces are beavers and maple leaves.

There is a dedicatory inscription on the face of the silver base. A view of the city of Montreal is engraved on the reverse side, while the remaining four panels reproduce elements of the arms of the city. The implied content is summarized in the address to Stephens, as reported in the press: "The moral of its symbolic teaching speaks for itself in the types of Justice, Vigilance and Honesty on the one hand; Industry, Commerce and Art on the other – the whole being suggestive of the great interests committed to your care, and which have hitherto received your protection."[17]

Weighted with a like symbolic content is the Mitchell epergne (Fig. 27). Another fine presentation piece by Hendery, it is of a somewhat more common type than the Stephens Testimonial, and recalls the Cartier centrepiece described earlier. The designer is not known. On one side of the triangular base is a portrait of the Honourable Peter Mitchell, surmounted by his coat-of-arms. On another is the dedication.

On the third side is an engraving of the town of Newcastle, showing the harbour, shipping, and particularly the last vessel (the 32nd) built by Mr. Mitchell, surmounted by the coat-of-arms of the Province of New Brunswick. The triangle is festooned above by a cable chain and a wreath of maple leaves. On a platform above this is a lighthouse, complete in everything, and beautifully fitted with reflectors, a capstan, rudder, fender, boathooks, oars, anchor, sail, block, tackle, &c. On the third corner of the pedestal is a stand with compass inside, quadrant, chart, telescope, and British and Dominion flags.[18]

The stem is in the form of a maple tree; the branches are bedecked with leaves and support alternating crystal dishes and candle sockets. The crowning element is a large crystal bowl. The whole stood about one metre high and the silver used weighed 580 ounces.[19]

As evidenced here, Naturalism still persists as a preferred style for epergnes and candelabra, although

26

27

26 Testimonial, designed by Felix Paris, and manufactured by Robert Hendery. A wood engraving in the *Canadian Illustrated News*, Montreal, 19 May 1877, p. 308.

27 Presentation epergne, manufactured by Robert Hendery. A wood engraving in the *Canadian Illustrated News*, Montreal, 19 September 1874, p. 180.

its use elsewhere is falling off. Hendery continues to adapt this essentially English style to suit the Canadian fancy, and again the maple substitutes for the customary oak or vine branches of English epergnes.

This testimonial was offered to the Honourable Peter Mitchell, M.P., by the constituents of his home riding of Northumberland County, New Brunswick, on 5 September 1874. Mitchell had been Minister of Marine and Fisheries from 1867 until 1873. This tribute occasioned another often-heard assertion of national pride on the part of the *Canadian Illustrated News* [Montreal] of 29 September 1874 (p. 18): "It is too common a custom to order articles for presentation from England when their cost exceeds a couple of hundred dollars. Mr. Hendery has shown that quite as good workmanship can be had in this country."

The Carslake Trophy (Fig. 28) is a splendid later example of sculpture in silver by Hendery & Leslie. John Leslie is said to have done the designing in the later years of the Hendery firms (see Appendix II), and it is possible that he was responsible for this piece. A trophy for regular competition between the regimental rifle teams of the active militia across Canada, it is named for George Carslake, the donor, and was to be awarded at the annual August matches of the Province of Quebec Rifle Association. Evidently the donor intended it to be the finest shooting trophy in Canada. With a height of 61 centimetres, it contained 160 ounces of silver. The *Montreal Gazette*, 7 May 1890 (p. 2), gives the following detailed description of the design:

Rising from a solid silver base fringed with acanthus leaves and plain burnished borders are six panels framed in ebony and left blank for inscriptions. This forms the pedestal proper. Above this is a delicately fashioned cylinder of ebony on which are hand burnished shields bearing the arms of the different provinces of Canada separated by sprays of maple leaves. Standing out from the shield are two stands of flags, surrounded by blank shields, and surmounted by the Royal Crown. A delicate tracery of ornamented bay leaves runs around the centre of the ebony portion, which curves gracefully inward and forms the base for what may be called the trophy proper. In this

there are six figures representing the divisions of the service, standing between spiral columns with Corinthian caps, and arched over with conventional acanthus. The panels separating the figures will be of polished ebony. Above this runs a fluted border on which stand six delicately designed urns, and rising from this base is a pedestal for the topmost figure. Canada is represented by the conventional female, holding aloft a maple leaf, while at her feet the beaver is seen.

The writer concludes: "It is one of the most magnificent trophies ever made in Canada."

The first winner of the Carslake Trophy was the rifle team of the Victoria Rifles of Canada (of Montreal) in the 1890 competition. In spite of the Hendery firms' long-proven ability to create large and impressive works of silver, most pieces of this type continue to be imported. Admittedly there was also a diminished demand by the century's end, as tastes changed.

Production of presentation silver in Canada was centred in Montreal, largely because of the Hendery firms, with very little activity elsewhere in the province. Quebec City, which traditionally boasted an active silver craft, still had in this half-century such silversmiths as François Sasseville, and his successors Pierre Lespérance (1819–1882) and Ambroise-Adhémar Lafrance (1847–1905). Most of their wares were destined primarily for the church, and only secondarily for table and other domestic purposes. They generally made very little in the way of presentation silver.

The situation in the Maritimes did not differ greatly. By the mid-1850s little silver was being made outside of Halifax, and even in that city the silversmiths were few. There was Peter Nordbeck (1789–1861), William Herman Newman (1826–1894), and Julius Cornelius (1825–1916), all German-born and -trained, and Michael Septimus Brown (1818–1886). However, the craft was very much in decline, and by the 1870s almost all presentation silver, as well as most large silver items, was being supplied by Hendery or by imports.

British Columbia and Manitoba were of too recent settlement for silversmithing to have taken hold. They shared the same basic sources of supply as the above-mentioned provinces, except that some of the silver imported into British Columbia came from San Francisco.

Evaluation of the situation in Upper Canada, later Ontario, is more difficult, as it is quite complex and has never been properly studied. At present it is not always possible to distinguish between the active silversmith and the retail silversmith. Toronto, as the chief metropolitan centre, attracted the major share of the industry, which by the end of the century was quite vigorous.

The confusion that confronts the student of Ontario silver comes into focus in the person of William C. Morrison (active c.1846–1890) of Toronto. Morrison is the reputed maker of a spade after a design (Fig. 29) by Kivas Tully (1820–1905), an Irish-born architect and engineer who settled in Toronto in 1844.[20] A sketch of this nature is an extreme rarity, and a document of great interest in the study of Canadian silver. Both design and spade are in the same private collection. The attribution of the spade to Morrison is problematic in that Morrison is often thought to have been only a retailer of silver. It is certain that he was a retailer in his later years; however, the spade was commissioned as early as 1851.

At this time there were few silversmiths in the entire country able to reproduce such a design – nor is it likely the work of an occasional silversmith. The question arises as to whether Morrison merely accepted the commission. And if this is the case, who was the local silversmith responsible for the expert craftsmanship? We can only presume it was made locally, as Tully's design is dated 30 August 1851, and the event for which the spade was intended occurred on 15 October of the same year. Aside from Richard Kestell Oliver, known mainly for his flatware, Morrison is the only person regularly listed as a silversmith in Toronto city directories of the 1850s. Henry Jackson was still in the city at this time, but he is listed as a watchmaker and jeweller. Furthermore, Morrison alone was a consistent winner of prizes for the "best specimens of silversmiths' work" at the Upper Canada Provincial Exhibitions, capturing the honours in 1852, 1856, and 1858. Did he make this spade?

Compelling in its subdued elegance, the design shows a maple leaf displayed prominently on the upper and under sides of the blade. It almost has the character

28

29

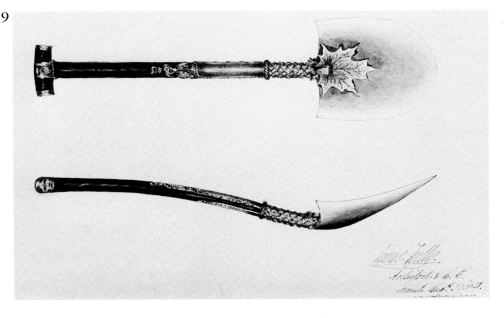

28 Design for the Carslake Trophy, executed by Hendery & Leslie for the Province of Quebec Rifle Association. A reproduction in the *Dominion Illustrated,* London, 10 May 1890, p. 295.

29 Sketch of a ceremonial spade for the Ontario, Simcoe & Huron Railroad Union Co. Drawing by Kivas Tully, 1851. 19 × 27.3 cm. Private collection.

41

30 Prize cups. A page from *The Toronto Silver Plate Company's Illustrated Catalogue and Price List of Electro Silver Plate*, 1888. From the left (each trophy is described as "chased, gold lined"): cricket cup, 40 cm high, $30; athletic cup, 50 cm high, $75; sporting cup, 37 cm high, $30.

31 "The Buffalo Hunt." Meriden Britannia Company, Meriden, Connecticut (or perhaps Meriden Britannia Company, Hamilton, Ontario), c.1882. Electroplate; 51 cm high. Musée du Québec (A-42.62-S).

of jewellery and admittedly Morrison was also a jeweller. The appearance of the maple leaf as a popular decorative motif on silver in this province is simultaneous with that in Lower Canada (cf. Fig. 20). The spade was used by Lady Elgin in the ceremonial turning of the first sod of the Ontario, Simcoe and Huron Railroad, at Toronto on 15 October 1851. Tully also designed an equally attractive wheelbarrow for the occasion.

J.G. Joseph & Co. of Toronto were the leading retail jewellers and silversmiths in Upper Canada in the late 1850s and 1860s, and their name is frequently associated with presentation silver. The business was founded by Judah George Joseph in 1842. Born in Exeter, England, in 1798, Joseph emigrated to the United States and settled in Cincinnati, Ohio, about 1829. It seems that he has sometimes been confused with Joseph G. Joseph (born 1812), silversmith of that same city, who was a probable business associate (and relative?). In any event, the J.G. Joseph who operated the "Spectacle Store" in Cincinnati until 1840 must have been Judah G. Joseph. That year Judah Joseph moved to Hamilton, and then in 1842 to Toronto. In Toronto, Joseph continued as an optician, mathematical instrument maker, and jeweller, among other things. No doubt he also worked in silver – that is, at the very least he must have engaged in the specialized work of making gold and silver spectacle frames. Of possible significance is the fact that the maker's mark given to Joseph G. Joseph of Cincinnati is very like (identical to?) one of several marks used by Judah G. Joseph in Toronto.[21] It is likely that the former mark actually belongs to Judah Joseph as well, and this circumstance in turn reinforces the probability that he also made flatware and other articles.

Judah Joseph died in 1857 and his business became J.G. Joseph & Co. under the direction of Henry J. Altman and Thomas H. Lee. By 1865 John F. Lash was taken into partnership. It has not been firmly established whether or not they made any silver. They did retail silver by a number of local silversmiths, as well as by Robert Hendery, and much American silver which they frequently re-marked. In 1871 the retail side of the business was ceded to John Lash, who formed Lash & Co. The firm J.G. Joseph & Co. continued as wholesale jewellers until its bankruptcy in October 1878, about

the same time as Savage, Lyman & Co. went into liquidation. Lash & Co. lasted only until about 1876.[22]

Another name that arises in conjunction with presentation silver is that of James E. Ellis (& Co.). Ellis came to Toronto from Liverpool, England, in 1848. Sometime before 1867 he took his son of the same name and Matthew T. Cain into partnership as James E. Ellis & Co., which becomes the J.E. Ellis Co., Ltd., by 1895. The firm ceases operation by 1902. Much of the presentation silver retailed by Ellis was imported from England. Like J.G. Joseph & Co. and William Morrison, Ellis sold Hendery silver.

Roden is also a name that merits mention. A Toronto-based manufacturer of silver and electroplate, the firm was founded in 1891 as Roden Bros. by Frank and Thomas Roden. By 1915 it was known as Roden Bros., Ltd., and continued under that name until 1953, when it was bought out by Henry Birks & Sons Limited.

Another significant dimension to the silver trade which emerges in the nineteenth century concerns electroplate (silverplate). Electroplating is a process whereby a base metal is coated with a thin layer of silver through the action of electricity. The product possesses the advantage of an appearance like silver, at only a fraction of the cost. It was G.R. Elkington of Birmingham, England, who in 1840 first successfully adapted the principle of electrodeposition to commercial use, and on a massive scale. Soon the process spread to Europe and the United States. In Canada electroplating was experimented with as early as 1850.[23] However, such endeavours were usually short-lived and for some time the Canadian industry remained small-scale, as it was unable to withstand the influx of wares from outside. The situation did not change substantially until 1879 when Prime Minister Sir John A. Macdonald succeeded in enacting a system of stringent protectionist tariffs as part of his "National Policy" for the development of Canadian industry.

As a counter-measure to the tariff, manufacturers of electroplate from the United States immediately began to set up branch factories in Canada. Heading the list is the Meriden Britannia Company of Meriden, Connecticut, which built a factory in Hamilton, Ontario, in 1879. Simpson, Hall, Miller & Co. of Wallingford, Connecticut, did likewise in Montreal that same year. Some Canadian-backed firms soon came into being, such as the Toronto Silver Plate Company, founded in 1882, which included trophies among its wide range of products (Fig. 30). Nevertheless, American firms dominated the production of electroplate, and during the last two decades of the nineteenth century Meriden Britannia Company of Hamilton, in particular, produced many rather important Canadian presentation pieces and trophies.

On 17 March 1882, the Marquis of Lorne, Governor-General of Canada, was presented with ''The Buffalo Hunt'' (Fig. 31), an electroplated sculptural group by the Meriden Britannia Company. Dr John C. Schultz, M.P., presented the piece on behalf of his constituents in Lisgar County, Manitoba. The purpose of the occasion was to commemorate Lord Lorne's official tour of western Canada the preceding summer and autumn. This tour extended through Manitoba and the prairies as far as the Rocky Mountains. It was an undertaking of momentous importance for the history of western Canada, as Lord Lorne was deeply impressed with the vast potential of this land, which had long been dismissed as sterile and hostile. His tour in effect became a great promotional crusade. Among other things, Lord Lorne made maximal use of the wide press coverage that the tour attracted. He also roused interest through his enthusiastic writings and public addresses, setting before Canadians and Britons alike an image of the Canadian West as a near paradise.

It would seem that the people of Lisgar County had chosen a thematically appropriate tribute to Lord Lorne's contribution to the development of the West; nevertheless, the piece was not created for the occasion. Rather it is a stock catalogue item of the Meriden Britannia Company.[24] The original was quite celebrated: designed by Theodore Baur and cast in bronze, it was first exhibited by the Meriden Britannia Company at the first great American exposition, the Philadelphia Centennial of 1876, and subsequently was shown at other expositions. It stood as a symbol for the passing of one era and the beginning of another, or the ''Winning of the West.'' Thus, with the Lorne presentation, the symbolic content of ''The Buffalo Hunt'' has been reaffirmed in a Canadian context.

The widespread popularity enjoyed by Baur's bronze led the Meriden Britannia Company to produce replicas in electroplate. Two types were made available: in

30

31

actual size or in a reduced version; in "old silver, gold inlaid" or "old silver." The Lorne testimonial is an example of an actual-size replica made in "old silver." As the designs of the American parent factory were accessible to the Canadian one, it is possible that the Lorne "Buffalo Hunt" was cast by Meriden Britannia Co. in Hamilton (now known as the International Silver Company of Canada, Ltd.).[25] In general, Canadian subsidiary factories were duplicates of their American parents. Even the original workmen in the Canadian factories came from the United States.[26]

Electroplate held a very large share of the market in presentation pieces and trophies during the late nineteenth century. As a low-cost substitute for silver, electroplate shared many of the designs and technical processes used in the production of sterling. From its inception in Canada many silversmiths engaged in electroplating, Robert Hendery being among the first. Unfortunately, today few of the earliest of these products can be identified. By the century's end, the manufacture of electroplate was generally concentrated in a few large enterprises. However, to this day both sectors of the silver trade continue to be closely allied, and in the study of silver design, electroplate cannot entirely be excluded.

Notes

1. In his wills of 1834 and 1837, George Savage Sr refers to Joseph as his partner. In his will of 1842, George Sr speaks of having given his concern in business over to Joseph. Archives nationales du Québec, Montreal: N.B. Doucet, Nos. 22138 (30 Dec. 1834) and 24487 (9 June 1837); E. Guy, No. 4915 (10 Dec. 1842).

2. R.W.S. Mackay, *The Montreal Directory for 1842–3* (Montreal: Lovell & Gibson & R.W.S. Mackay, 1842), p. 219.

3. National Gallery of Canada, Curatorial Archives, Letter of P.W. Wood to H. Birks, 7 Dec. 1904.

4. *Montreal Gazette*, 7 Oct. 1878, p. 1; 8 Oct. 1878, p. 1; 23 Oct. 1878, p. 1; 13 Nov. 1878, pp. 1, 2; etc.

5. *Canadian Illustrated News* [Montreal], 21 Dec. 1878, p. 398.

6. *Montreal Transcript*, 8 Oct. 1859, p. 2.

7. Some Savage sources: Archives nationales du Québec, Montreal, Registers of Zion (Congregational) Church; *Montreal Transcript*, 26 Dec. 1863, p. 2; *Canadian Illustrated News* [Montreal], 25 Dec. 1875, pp. 403, 412; F.J. Britten, *Old Clocks and Watches & Their Makers*, 5th ed., rev. (London: E. & F.N. Spon, Limited, 1922), p. 772; G.E. Burrows, *Canadian Clocks*

8. *Montreal Transcript*, 8 Mar. 1855, p. 2; *Canada at the Universal Exhibition of 1855*, pp. 189, 403.

9. Some Hendery sources: Archives nationales du Québec, Montreal, Registers of St Gabriel Street (Presbyterian) Church and Registers of St George's (Anglican) Church; Public Archives Canada, Canada Census 1861 and 1871; J.E. Langdon, *Canadian Silversmiths & Their Marks 1667–1867* (Lunenburg, Vt.: The Stinehour Press, 1960), pp. 137–140; R. Boily, *Monnaies, médailles et jetons au Canada* (Quebec: La Société numismatique de Québec, 1980), pp. 37–40.

10. *Montreal Gazette*, 23 Sept. 1863, p. 2.

11. *Montreal Transcript*, 3 Jan. 1863, p. 2.

12. *Illustrated London News*, 3 Aug. 1850, p. 97; J. Culme, *Nineteenth-Century Silver* (London: Country Life Books, 1977), p. 120; P. Wardle, *Victorian Silver and Silver-Plate* (London: Herbert Jenkins, 1963), p. 93.

13. *Canadian Illustrated News* [Montreal], 21 Sept. 1872, pp. 179–181.

14. *Montreal Transcript*, 29 May 1858, p. 2.

15. National Gallery of Canada, Curatorial Archives, Notes of W.F. Denman, Feb. 1939; also Montreal city directories.

16. It is not known where in England he came from. Could he possibly be related to the retail silversmith T.J. Paris of Liverpool?

17. *Canadian Illustrated News* [Montreal], 19 May 1877, pp. 308–310.

18. *Canadian Illustrated News* [Montreal], 29 Sept. 1874, p. 180.

19. *St. John Daily News*, 7 Sept. 1874, p. 2.

20. R. Strong, *A Pageant of Canada*, exhibition catalogue (Ottawa: National Gallery of Canada, 1967), pp. 296–297.

21. Cf. E.D. Beckman, *Cincinnati Silversmiths, Jewelers, Watch and Clockmakers* (Cincinnati: B.B. & Co., 1975), p. 75; and J.E. Langdon, *Guide to Marks on Early Canadian Silver* (Toronto: The Ryerson Press, 1968), p. 41.

22. Some Joseph sources: *Weekly Colonist* [Toronto], 29 May 1857, p. 2; *Canadian Illustrated News* [Montreal], 22 June 1872, p. 387; S.A. Speisman, *The Jews of Toronto: A History to 1937* (Toronto: McClelland and Stewart, 1979), pp. 12–13, 16-17, ff.; Beckman, *Cincinnati Silversmiths*, pp. 74-76.

23. J.E. Langdon, "Silver and Silverplate," *Canadian Collector*, X (Sept./Oct. 1975), p. 60.

24. *The Meriden Britannia Silver-Plate Treasury: The Complete Catalog of 1886–7*, Introduction by E.P. Hogan (New York: Dover Publications, Inc., 1982), pp. 3, 10.

25. *Daily Citizen* [Ottawa], 18 Mar. 1882, p. 1; *Manitoba Free Press* [Winnipeg], 21 Mar. 1882, p. 1; *Canadian Illustrated News* [Montreal], 8 Apr. 1882, pp. 211, 217; D.T. and H.I. Rainwater, *American Silverplate* (Nashville, Tenn.: Thomas Nelson, Inc., 1968), pp. 137–140; P.J. Broder, *Bronzes of the American West* (New York: Harry N. Abrams, Inc. [c.1974]), pp. 256–258.

26. "Jewellery and Silverware," *Industrial Canada*, V (June 1905), pp. 760–761.

Chapter IV

32 Claret jug and pair of goblets. Maker's mark of Robert Hendery for Savage & Lyman, c.1859. Silver, one goblet (27756) gilt lined; 28.2 cm high (jug). Birks (27754–27756).

1850–1899: Presentation Pieces

The second half of the nineteenth century is the period for which the Birks Collection has the richest variety of presentation pieces and trophies – a period which is also the heyday for this type of silver in Canada. Nonetheless there are certain gaps in the collection. Noticeably lacking are monumental works or examples of silver sculpture, as discussed in the previous chapter.

Among the larger and more interesting pieces, both from an aesthetic and an historical point of view, are four pitchers, either alone or as part of a set with goblets, and, in one instance, with a tray. Robert Hendery is the maker of all the pieces and Savage & Lyman the retailer. In fact, there is a preponderance of works by these two firms in the collection. The imbalance arises from the original raison d'être of the Henry Birks Collection – namely, to amass works by the Montreal antecedents of Henry Birks & Sons Limited. For this reason as well, there are disproportionately few works from Ontario.

Of earliest date, c.1859, are a claret jug and two goblets by Robert Hendery for Savage & Lyman (Fig. 32). The presentation theme is a political one, concerning the righting of an election fraud, and the hero of the occasion is the Honourable Philip Henry Moore, Member of the Legislative Council of United Canada from 1841 until 1867. When the municipal election was held on 27 January 1858 in the township of Dunham, Missisquoi County, Quebec, the incumbent councillors foresaw that they would not be re-elected, as indeed proved to be the case. Accordingly, they resorted to some prearranged chicanery to have the election nullified. The returning officer, citing some irregularities for which he himself was actually responsible, was able to report to the provincial (United Canada) government that in effect no election had taken place. This, in turn, enabled the provincial government to use a legal loophole to reinstate the former councillors, despite the protests of the outraged electors who were thus deprived of their franchise.

Moore, who was from Missisquoi County, pressed the government for an investigation, but with no imme-

diate result. Eventually the affair was settled in court in favour of the Dunham ratepayers. In gratitude for his support, they presented Moore with this claret set in January 1859. At the time it also included a tray.[1] Of a design that is common for English examples of that date, the jug has an embossed and chased all-over ornament of vine leaves and grapes, C-scrolls by the spout, a vine stem for a handle, and a grape finial on the cover.

From the same year is another service with water pitcher, six goblets, and tray, by Hendery for Savage & Lyman (Fig. 33). The inscription on the tray reads: *This Tray, / with Jug & 6 Cups / is Presented to / DAVID STARK ESQ^R / by the Employees on the / MONTREAL & ISLAND POND DISTRICT OF THE GRAND TRUNK RAILWAY. / as a token of their Respect & Esteem, on his / Resigning the Superintendence of that Division. / SHERBROOKE. / JULY 1859.* The jug is similarly inscribed. The *Montreal Gazette*, 30 July 1859 (p. 2) describes the ornament: "The jug is of the Hebe form, in the front is engraved the inscription (which is very well executed), in a shield formed by the grouping of maple trees.... Around the edge of the lip, as well as the base, is a wreath of maple leaves, while the handle is composed of boughs entwined." The body proper has a pictorial aspect, as do the cups of the goblets, which have been etched, chased, and embossed with various railroad scenes. Realistic depictions such as these were quite fashionable in Britain and the United States. The Stark service represents a very early Canadian attempt of this kind. Needless to say this treatment demanded a certain virtuosity, even though the results are slightly prosaic, and suggests the hand of a specialized silverchaser. Could this be the work of Felix Paris?

On one side of the pitcher is a scene showing (as described by the Montreal *Pilot*): "the Chaudière Iron Bridge, near Quebec, the river and rapids below being well delineated, a train passing over the bridge" (Fig. 34). This bridge, completed a few years earlier, was located just upstream from the famed Chaudière

Falls. It was on the old Quebec and Richmond Railway section of the Grand Trunk Railway. On the other side of the pitcher is "a view of another bridge on the Portland section of the road, of one span, the abutments and trees near it beautifully brought out" (Fig. 35). This scene is supposed to represent the Grand Trunk bridge which spanned the Richelieu River at Belœil, with Mount Saint-Hilaire (also Mount Belœil) visible in the background.[2] If that is the case, it is a somewhat naïve interpretation. The cup of each goblet reproduces a different scene from the Montreal and Island Pond section of the Grand Trunk, formerly the St Lawrence and Atlantic Railroad. The set serves as a marvellous early visual record of that railway, which ran from Montreal through St-Hyacinthe, Richmond, and Sherbrooke, to Island Pond, Vermont.

The third pitcher by Robert Hendery for Savage & Lyman (Fig. 36) in the Birks Collection is of special interest largely because of the recipient and the nature of the presentation, as otherwise it is an unexceptional piece. The pitcher was given to Mrs James Sadlier by the St Patrick's Literary Association in Montreal in early May 1860. The ill-fated Thomas D'Arcy McGee, M.P., soon to die at the hands of an assassin, was president of that society, and chief among those honouring Mrs Sadlier. The presentation was occasioned by Mrs Sadlier's departure for New York where she was to take up residence.[3]

In her own time, Mrs Sadlier was a well-known author. Her literary accomplishments include some sixty novels dealing with Irish life, both in America and Ireland. Although commonly associated with the United States, she lived for a long time in Canada and did much of her writing here. Born Mary Anne Madden in County Cavan, Ireland, in 1820, she emigrated to Montreal in 1844. There she married James Sadlier in 1846. Sadlier was a principal partner in D. & J. Sadlier & Co., and was in charge of the Montreal branch of this New York-based publishing house, which would soon be the leading Catholic book publisher in the United States. In 1860 the Sadliers moved to New York, but maintained close contacts with Montreal, and both continued to be intimate friends of D'Arcy McGee. Following McGee's death in April 1868, Mrs Sadlier edited a book of his poems, which was published by her husband in 1869. James Sadlier died that same year.

32

33

34

35
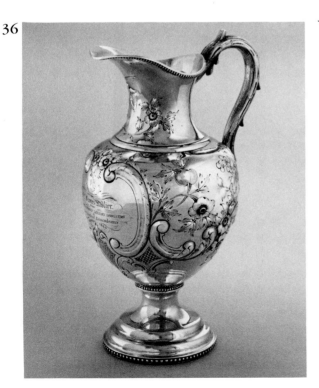

36

Mrs Sadlier returned to Montreal in 1880 and died there in 1903.

In the ornament on the Sadlier pitcher, there is an appropriate play of symbols evoking national sentiments. Such a treatment is characteristic of the age and in fact here it is quite temperate. Fixed conspicuously under the spout is a harp with plume above, which is the crest of the St Patrick's Literary Association. On the back of the body, by the handle, are sprays of shamrocks and maple leaves. Care has been taken to wed Irish emblems to Canadian ones, and they become Canadian as well as Irish. Anemones on the sides complete the floral ornament, and the inscription on the front is framed by C-scrolls with small panels of diaper-work and imbrication below. Although it incorporates Naturalism in the floral and foliate ornament, as well as the branch-like handle, this pitcher is more representative of the Rococo Revival style, which entered Canada in the 1820s and was at the height of popularity in the 1850s and 1860s.

All three pitchers discussed in the foregoing paragraphs are testimonials of a public nature – that is, a large number of people were involved in the presentation in one way or another. They were purchased through fairly wide subscription, or at least the presentation was a public event, and they commemorate some achievement of significance or interest to the community. In effect, they are a kind of portable public monument, whether acknowledging the achievements of a distinguished politician, business person, or literary figure. The fourth pitcher (Fig. 37) is a tribute of more personal import; again, it was made by Robert Hendery for Savage & Lyman.

The precise nature of the occasion has not been determined, but in this instance the presentation was made by four sisters. The inscription reads: *PRESENTED TO / John Boston Esq͏ʳ. / BY / ELEANOR JULIA ESTHER & ELIZABETH PHILLIPS / as a small token of / GRATITUDE / MONTREAL 22ⁿᵈ OCT͏ʳ. / 1861*. The four sisters were all daughters of Thomas Phillips, a prominent Montreal businessman, best known as one of the contractors for the Rideau Canal. John Boston was Sheriff of Montreal from 1839 until 1862. Born in Scotland, he died in Montreal on 8 March 1862 at about seventy-five years of age.

The key to explaining this presentation may rest with

33 Water pitcher, six goblets, and tray. Maker's mark of Robert Hendery for Savage & Lyman, 1859. Silver, goblets gilt lined; 35 cm high (pitcher). Birks (26097–26104).

34 Water pitcher in Fig. 33, with scene of the Chaudière bridge of the Grand Trunk Railway. Maker's mark of Robert Hendery for Savage & Lyman, 1859. Silver; 35 cm high. Birks (26097).

35 View of the Richelieu bridge of the Grand Trunk Railway at Belœil, Quebec. Detail (opposite side) of water pitcher shown in Fig. 34.

36 Pitcher. Maker's mark of Robert Hendery for Savage & Lyman, 1860. Silver; 28.3 cm high. Birks (25135).

37 Pitcher, with a view of St Andrew's Church, Beaver Hall Hill, Montreal. Maker's mark of Robert Hendery for Savage & Lyman, 1861. Silver; 34.5 cm high. Birks (25139).

38 View of Beaver Hall, Montreal. Detail, opposite side of pitcher in Fig. 37.

39 View of the Church of the Messiah and Beaver Hall Hill, Montreal. Detail of pitcher in Fig. 37.

the two etched and chased architectural scenes on the sides of the piece. As with the Stark and Sadlier pitchers, it would seem reasonably certain that this was a custom design to suit the occasion. One of the scenes is of special historical interest, as it is the best known illustration of Beaver Hall, an early Montreal landmark that disappeared long ago (Fig. 38).[4] Beaver Hall was the country home of Joseph Frobisher, or as Lady Simcoe called it, "Mr. Frobisher's villa on the side of the mountain [Mount Royal],"[5] and was located on what is now known as Beaver Hall Hill. Frobisher (1740–1810) was an original member of the North West Company, and a partner of Simon McTavish in McTavish, Frobisher and Company. He made a fortune in the fur trade and in his time was one of the wealthiest men in Canada.

When Frobisher retired in 1798, he made Beaver Hall his principal residence. It was situated on a forty-acre estate with large gardens, an orchard, and woods. This house is frequently referred to as a mansion by later writers; however, as this pitcher demonstrates, it was a rather unpretentious though large dwelling. A frame structure, or at least covered with clapboard siding, it measured 27 by 11 metres. The size of the interior can be surmised from a description of 1844, which mentions a drawing room, dining room, parlour, two kitchens, and fourteen bedrooms which could be increased to twenty. It is known to have been splendidly furnished when Frobisher lived there. Much later, Beaver Hall came into the possession of Thomas Phillips, who lived there for a number of years. The house burned down in 1847.

The depiction of Beaver Hall on this pitcher must be based on a sketch executed before 1843. Thomas Phillips died in 1842, and in 1843 the whole character of the estate began to alter as the Phillips heirs had new streets opened through it, parcelling the land into building lots which they put up for sale. One of these new streets was called Beaver Hall Hill. This illustration also shows Beaver Hall with modifications that were made to it only after the Phillips's occupancy. Originally, the main entrance to the house was on the north side and the orchard was in the back on the south side. Phillips reversed this orientation, as it appears on the ewer, by adding (or enlarging?) at least one doorway, the large one with the small portico, on the south

side. The curved driveway which opens at the gateway onto Lagauchetière Street was also new.[6]

Apparently the left curve of the driveway conformed approximately to that of present-day Beaver Hall Hill where it meets Lagauchetière. Beaver Hall itself would have been situated on the east side of Beaver Hall Hill, more or less opposite Belmont Street, or slightly lower. In May 1845, the Unitarian congregation dedicated its first church in Montreal on the site immediately in front of Beaver Hall. Therein lies the relationship to the scene on the other side of the pitcher. Together they represent a type of before-and-after sequence. Each shows the southernmost extremity of the old Frobisher estate, the one as it was in the 1820s or 1830s, the other as it was about 1858–61.

In the second scene (Fig. 39), the church on the right is the second Unitarian church, or the Church of the Messiah, which was built on the site of the first church and completed in 1858. As the second church was much larger, it probably overlapped onto the original site of Beaver Hall. The other church at the northwest corner of Lagauchetière Street and Beaver Hall Hill is St Andrew's Church (the Presbyterian Church of Canada, in connection with the Church of Scotland), which opened for worship in January 1851 (see Fig. 37 for detail of church). The artist has also been careful to render in the background the slender spire of Christ Church (Anglican) Cathedral, which was completed in 1858. Why this pitcher juxtaposes a cityscape with these churches and a former residence of the four donors remains a mystery. Sheriff Boston was an active member of one of the churches, St Andrew's. A suggestion of intimate friendship prevails.

These scenes are executed in a marvellously realistic manner, as is a wreath of naturalistic, chased vine leaves which encircles the inscription on the front of the body. Similar leaves, cast and applied, reach out from the branchlike handle and cling about the neck of the jug. A few other leaves also cluster about the lower handle join. The technique of the leaves is reminiscent of that of the maple leaves on the earlier tea and coffee service by Bohle & Hendery (Fig. 21). As a final touch, a small beaver finial tops the domed lid. This pitcher is another fine example of Naturalism in silver design, although now wedded with a classical urn form.

37

38

39

Apart from these pitchers and sets, the only other large item in the Birks Collection from this era is a tray by Robert Hendery & Co. (Fig. 40). The tray is oval in form, with applied ovolo rim and four anthemion feet; an engraved frieze of acanthus leaves, flowers, and strapwork surrounds the outer well or bottom. Stylistically this tray is Renaissance Revival. The inscription on the inside indicates it was offered to Mr and Mrs J.J. Gibb by a group of clergymen of the anglican diocese of Montreal on 23 April 1867: *With a respectful acknowledgement of / many services rendered by them / to the Church.*

Drinking vessels of relatively modest design, whether goblets, beakers, or children's cups, are the most popular form of presentation piece. There are a number of these in the Birks Collection. A presentation goblet received by Assistant Commissary General Alfred Salwey is typical, with its oviform cup, tall stem, and circular spreading foot (Fig. 41). It is absolutely chaste except for the engraved inscription with the Salwey crest above. Made by Robert Hendery for Savage & Lyman, it was: *Presented to / Assistant Commissary General Salwey. / By the Members of / The Commissariat Mess. / MONTREAL, / 1859.* Salwey was stationed at Montreal with the Commissariat Department from about 1857 until 1859. He retired from the British Army in 1863.

Two kiddush goblets by Robert Hendery & Co. are somewhat uncommon in that they are very early Canadian examples of Jewish ritual silver (Fig. 42). The kiddush is a ceremony of sanctification for welcoming the Sabbath, and it takes place in the home on Friday evening after the family returns from the service in the synagogue. Part of the ceremony requires a blessing over a cup of wine, from which everyone takes a drink. This cup of blessing is known as a kiddush cup.

Jewish ritual requires that the cup, especially the rim, be free of flaws. Hence, silver has traditionally been the preferred medium. Inscriptions such as biblical quotations, or religious motifs, are often found on these cups, though not necessarily. In these pieces the ornament is quite secular.[7] The oviform cup is chased with a scrolled foliate reserve on front and back (the front one with inscription) and a pendant floral spray on each side. Small panels of imbrication above complete the ornamental scheme.

These goblets were presented to Edward Moss on 2 August 1869 by the Congregation of English, German, and Polish Jews (later Congregation Shaar Hashomayim) in Montreal. Edward Moss, with his brothers David and Lawrence, had been a founder and longtime leader of that congregation, and all three contributed generously to the building of the synagogue, which was consecrated on 22 May 1860, and was the first practising the Ashkenazic ritual in British North America.[8] The Mosses were natives of England and had settled in Montreal sometime before 1842, where they were successful wholesale clothiers and furriers. In 1869 Edward Moss returned to his native country, where he died in 1876. He was presented with the kiddush goblets before his departure, as a sign of gratitude for his support of the Montreal congregation. When his brother David returned to England four years earlier, the congregation had acknowledged him similarly with a silver tea and coffee service.[9]

The Birks Collection embraces a number of smaller articles (goblets can also be included in this category), which are best described as presentation pieces of an intimate nature. Most are gifts that have been inscribed to commemorate some personal event in the lives of relatives or friends. The two major subdivisions of these articles are wedding gifts and children's cups.

Wedding gifts include the greatest range of articles. A fish slice and fork with the mark of Savage & Lyman (Fig. 43) is an example. "Fish carvers" was the more proper designation for such a set in the nineteenth century. The blade of the slice is etched and engraved with foliate and scroll ornament, and has small piercings (drains), which frame a motif of two crossed fish. Similar foliate ornament is found on the curved base and prongs of the fork. The upper handle of the fish slice bears this inscription: *Presented / 15!ʰ Nov 1866. / TO / Elly Elliott / on her Marriage with / J. Patterson Esq / as a slight token / OF LOVE / By her Uncle / H.L Renny / Lieut of the Corps of / Royal Engineers / Retired List.* Ellen Elliott of Montreal was the bride. Her father, Joseph Elliott, was at one time Secretary and Treasurer of the Grand Trunk Railway. The groom was James Patterson, an Irish immigrant, and clerk in the Office of the Auditor General at Ottawa. In 1878 he was promoted to Assistant Auditor General, a post he held for twelve years. The marriage

40

41

42

40 Tray. Maker's mark of Robert Hendery & Co., c.1867. Silver; 40.6 cm long. Birks (24126).

41 Goblet. Maker's mark of Robert Hendery for Savage & Lyman, c.1859. Silver; 19.2 cm high. Birks (24138).

42 Pair of kiddush goblets. Maker's mark of Robert Hendery & Co., c.1869. Silver, gilt lined; 17.1 cm high. Birks (24137 and 25134).

43 Pair of fish carvers. Mark of Savage & Lyman, c.1866. Silver; 33.3 cm long (fish slice). Birks (25967 and 25968).

44 Beaker. Maker's mark of François Sasseville, c.1862. Silver, gilt lined; 10.7 cm high. Birks (27767).

45 Child's cup. Maker's mark of Robert Hendery for Savage & Lyman, c.1860. Silver; 11.9 cm high. Birks (25208).

of this couple took place at St George's (Anglican) Church, Montreal. The officiant was the Reverend Canon William B. Bond, later Archbishop of Montreal and Primate of all Canada. He was assisted by the Reverend Edward Sullivan, later Bishop of Algoma.[10]

A beaker (Fig. 44) by François Sasseville has similar allusions to a "who's who." It is inscribed: *Présenté à / Mademoiselle Josephine Caron / le jour de son mariage / le 23 Juin 1862 / PAR / L.G. Baillairgé.* The bride was Marie-Louise-Joséphine, eldest daughter of the Honourable René-Édouard Caron, then a Judge of the Court of Queen's Bench. The father had a distinguished career as a jurist and politician, holding various public offices, among them: Mayor of Quebec City, 1834–1836 and 1840–1846; Member of the Legislative Council of United Canada (appointed 1841); and Lieutenant-Governor of Quebec 1873–1876. Caron was also a close friend and professional associate of Louis de Gonzague Baillairgé, the giver of the beaker; this would explain the latter's relationship to the bride.

A member of the famous Baillairgé family of Quebec architects and sculptors, Louis de Gonzague was the son of Pierre-Florent, and the grandson of Jean Baillairgé. The young Baillairgé studied law under Caron, and in 1844 became his partner. In 1850 both were appointed joint attorneys for the corporation of Quebec City. Their partnership was dissolved in 1853, when Caron was appointed Judge of the Superior Court of Lower Canada. Baillairgé remained as attorney for the corporation of the city, and also continued private practice. He was a founder and for fifteen years president of the Société Saint-Jean-Baptiste de Québec, and during his later years especially was very much of a philanthropist, favouring religious and educational endeavours.

The interconnection of distinguished names does not cease here. The groom was Jean-Thomas Taschereau, Q.C., Assistant Judge of the Superior Court of Lower Canada, and later Judge of the Supreme Court of Canada. This was his second marriage. The officiant was the brother of the groom, the Reverend Elzéar-Alexandre Taschereau, Rector of Laval University, and later Archbishop of Quebec and a Cardinal.[11]

The beaker given to the bride by L. de G. Baillairgé is a plain cylindrical form with only the slightest taper and with the inscription as its sole ornament. Yet this

very chasteness conveys a suggestion of elegance. In fact, this piece reproduces an English type of the period from 1790 to 1820; mid-Victorian Canadian examples usually have a lip and basal moulding, if not other ornament. Moreover, unlike most drinking vessels of this period, which were at least partially machine-made, this beaker was entirely handwrought. Closer observation also indicates its substantiality, as it has been made from a heavy gauge of silver. By contrast, Hendery's beakers or cups are often quite thin-walled.

Sasseville was one of several silversmiths working in Quebec City in the later nineteenth century who adhered to traditional craft methods, and even designs, which were largely abandoned elsewhere in Canada. Not that he excluded the use of innovative techniques: quite the contrary. But his use of such techniques depended on the nature of the piece. His works produced in a traditional manner frequently reveal an innately superior quality, even when of very simple design. It is a quality that can only be fully appreciated through first-hand examination and comparison with other contemporary works.

Children's silver forms another category of presentation silver of a personal nature. Small cups or mugs are the most numerous. Today these are usually referred to as christening or baby cups, but these terms are something of a misnomer. In the Victorian period the cups had multiple uses and were sometimes even presented to adults. True, their most frequent use was as children's christening or birthday gifts. However, it is difficult to establish the precise purpose of most of the examples, as so many do not have any inscription, and when they do, it often consists of no more than a first name or initials. In addition, small beakers and occasionally even porringers serve the same functions and often substitute for cups.

There are dozens of examples of children's cups in the Birks Collection (Figs. 45–49). They assume a vast range of shapes and ornament; however, the most popular style is the Rococo Revival. In this style, the forms are usually cylindrical or bulbous and pear-shaped, and the ornament is usually chased, consisting of C-scrolls and floral sprays. Handles are generally cast, and in C-scroll or S-scroll forms. One such example by Robert Hendery for Savage & Lyman (Fig. 45) is inscribed: *Presented / TO / Effie Lucia Clara / by*

43

44

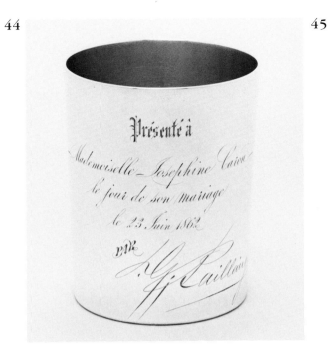

45

ber / Godfather, / 1ˢᵗ Janʸ 1860. From the date it can be conjectured that this might be a New Year's rather than a christening gift. Another mug with the mark of Savage & Lyman (Fig. 46) has the inscription: *William B. Nivin. / A. BIRTHDAY GIFT / June 30ᵗʰ / 1864.* William Bourne Nivin, the son of Montreal merchant William Nivin, was born on 30 June 1860.[12] He was therefore four years old when he received this mug.

A more distinctly Quebec design is seen in a cup by Pierre Lespérance (Fig. 48). Tumblers of this size and shape were very popular in Lower Canada throughout the eighteenth century and were used for drinking spirits. When they were later out of fashion they were sometimes converted into children's cups by the addition of a handle. Presumably, most of these adaptations date from the nineteenth century. Here Lespérance has reproduced a cup of this type. The tumbler section was formed by raising or shaping a disc of silver in the traditional manner; however, ironically enough in light of the prototype, an old English spoon-handle was worked into the scrolled handle of the cup. The underside of the handle still has London hallmarks for 1807–08. In contrast to the customarily plain exterior of the prototype, Lespérance has engraved a delicate floral garland on two sides, and a shaped shield on front, which contains the name "Alice." Inscribed under the bottom is: *1ᵉʳ Janʳ 1869.*

Ambroise Lafrance, also of Quebec City, made cups of traditional design of which there are several examples in the Birks Collection. One is a bulbous, almost barrel-form cup (Fig. 49) that recalls English types of the turn of the eighteenth century. Lafrance forgoes any ornament on this piece save the monogram "BMT" engraved on the front. In its stark simplicity and heavy gauge it is reminiscent of works by François Sasseville who, with Lespérance, had been Lafrance's master (cf. Fig. 44).

Beakers were often substituted for cups and are similarly inscribed. A footed beaker in the form of a thistle, by Robert Hendery for Savage & Lyman, is an example (Fig. 50). The inscription indicates it was given to Sidney H. Holmes by his godfather "W.M.M.". Because of the design of the cup, one might assume that young Holmes was of Scottish blood. The thistle as a motif, and a form, was used in almost every imaginable way in silver by the Royal Scotch Jewellery Com-

46

47

48

50

49

46 Mug. Mark of Savage & Lyman, c.1864. Silver, gilt lined; 9.4 cm high. Birks (25209).

47 Mug. Mark of Lash & Co., c.1871–76. Silver; 8.3 cm high. Birks (25192).

48 Child's cup. Maker's mark of Pierre Lespérance, c.1869. Silver; 6.6 cm high. Birks (27753).

49 Child's cup. Maker's mark of Ambroise-Adhémar Lafrance, c.1870–90. Silver, gilt lined; 8.3 cm high. Birks (24087).

50 Beaker. Maker's mark of Robert Hendery for Savage & Lyman, c.1860–65. Silver, gilt lined; 10.7 cm high. Birks (27757).

51 Porringer. Maker's mark of Robert Hendery, c.1863. Silver; 24.3 cm long. Birks (25050).

52 Trowel. Mark of P. Poulin & Son, c.1871. Silver; 30 cm long. Birks (25137).

53 Blade of trowel in Fig. 52.

pany of Edinburgh and London, which had every desire of furthering recognition of the thistle as a national emblem of Scotland.[13] Hendery was no doubt familiar with these or similar products of other Scottish manufacturing silversmiths.

Occasionally in the late nineteenth century, porringers were also given to children. In retrospect this is somewhat unusual, as traditionally the porringer (or bleeding bowl, as it was known in England) was a vessel rarely made by Canadian silversmiths. In that sense colonial Canadian tastes mirrored those of the English, for by the time of British rule in Canada, beginning in 1759, the form was uncommon in England. The situation in the United States was dissimilar, as the porringer was in common use throughout the eighteenth century, though at that time it was not meant specifically for children. Its later appearance in Canada is as an adoption of the American custom, then current, of giving porringers to children.

The Birks Collection has such a porringer by Robert Hendery (Fig. 51), which in fact reproduces a well-known eighteenth-century American type with "keyhole" handle.[14] These words are engraved on the front of the bowl: *To Harry FROM Aunt Anna / September 9th 1863.* Harry is Henry Hunt Hogan, whose initials "H.H.H." are also found on the handle. Presumably, Aunt Anna is Anna Workman. The Hogan and Workman families were well-to-do Irish Unitarians who lived in Montreal. Young Harry was the eldest son of Henry Hogan, owner of St Lawrence Hall, which was then and for the next several decades Montreal's finest hotel. Henry Jr was born in 1862, and the porringer was a gift for his first birthday.

A final group of silver articles that falls within the scope of this chapter comprises small commemorative pieces used in celebrating public inaugurations of one kind or another. Trowels for laying the cornerstones of buildings are in this category. In Canada, such trowels were being used by the 1840s (cf. Fig. 18), and were very popular throughout the second half of the century. The inscription on the blade of a trowel (Figs. 52 and 53) with the mark[15] of P. Poulin & Son (Pierre E. Poulin and Jacques D. Poulin, active c.1858–1875) of Quebec City, explains the nature of the event for which it was intended – the laying of the cornerstone of the Post Office in Quebec City, 17 July 1871.[16]

Engraved above the inscription are the Arms of Canada as they existed at the time. In fact these arms were not official, as it was only in 1921 that the Dominion of Canada was granted armorial bearings by Royal proclamation. To remedy this lack in the long interim period beginning in 1867, the Canadian government simply borrowed the design of the Great Seal of Canada for the Arms of Canada. This design was granted by a Royal Warrant issued by Queen Victoria on 26 May 1868, and consisted of a shield bearing quarterly the arms of the four original provinces of Canada – Ontario, Quebec, New Brunswick, and Nova Scotia. The arms on the trowel are those used from about 1868 until 1870–71; they were modified when British Columbia entered Confederation in 1870 and Manitoba in 1871 by the addition of the arms of these new provinces, and again later on by those of any new province.[17] The engraver has ensigned these early arms with a Royal Crown and wreathed them with maple leaves. A curious feature appears in the upper quarters containing the arms of Ontario and Quebec, where shamrocks have been substituted for maple leaves. Dominating this blade is the large, cast, beaver handle. Sir Hector-Louis Langevin, Minister of Public Works for Canada (1869–1873 and 1879–1891), was the recipient of this piece.

Another trowel, which has a wooden handle and an almost diamond-shaped blade with engraved rinceau border (Fig. 54), was made by Robert Hendery for William H. Tracy (active c.1864–1892) of Ottawa.[18] The blade is inscribed in this manner: *PRESENTED / TO / Miss Bella McGee, / by the Trustees of / Wesleyan Methodist Church / of Stittsville / ON THE OCCASION OF / Laying the Corner Stone / 2nd JULY 1883.* Miss McGee was the daughter of W.H. McGee of Merrickville, Ontario.[19]

Among other small inaugural pieces is a railway spike (Fig. 55) said to have been made by Albert Dumouchel when working for Hendery & Leslie.[20] Following the completion of the second and last segment of the United Counties Railway, which ran from Iberville through St-Hyacinthe to Bellevue Junction (near Sorel), Quebec, the ceremonial opening of the entire railway was celebrated. The Honourable Joseph-Adolphe Chapleau officiated.[21] He was presented with this silver spike, which is suitably engraved: *Souvenir de*

51

53

52

54 Trowel with turned wooden handle. Maker's mark of Robert Hendery for William H. Tracy, c.1883. Silver; 26 cm long. Birks (25138).

l'Inauguration du Chemin de fer des Comtés- 54 *Unis / Samedi, neuf Février 1895. / A l'honorable J.A. Chapleau, / Lieutenant-Gouverneur de la Province de Québec.*

Chapleau also presided at the opening of the Quebec Winter Carnival of 1896, and was presented with a silver ceremonial key (Fig. 56) to the "Ice Palace" or "Phare de glace" by Simon-Napoléon Parent, Mayor of Quebec City and later Premier of Quebec.[22] This ice structure was erected on the ramparts opposite the Legislative Assembly, and a representation of it is engraved on the web of the key. Attached to the looped handle-end is a shield bearing this inscription: *Souvenir du Carnaval / de Québec 1896 / OFFERT AU / Lt. Gouverneur / L'Hon. J.A. Chapleau / PAR / le Comité executif / a l'occasion de l'ouverture du / Palais de glace.* Cyrille Duquet (1841–1922), watchmaker, jeweller, and silversmith of Quebec City was the maker.

Unique presentation pieces such as these – whether they honour members of legislative councils, literary figures, religious leaders or jurists, or commemorate the inauguration of railways, public buildings or festivals – all speak to us about people in the throes of building a country. They are thus a record not only of the growth and refining of the art of silver-making, but also, in their way, part of the myriad symbols and events that go toward the shaping of a nation.

55

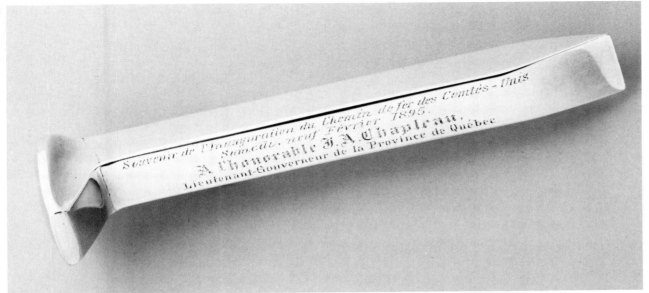

56

55 Railway spike. Attributed to Albert Dumouchel as workman for Hendery & Leslie, c.1895. Silver; 14 cm long. Birks (25143).

56 Ceremonial key. Maker's mark of Cyrille Duquet, c.1896. Silver; 16.7 cm long. Birks (25144).

Notes

1. *Advertiser* [Waterloo, Que.], 20 Jan. 1859, p. 2.
2. *Pilot* [Montreal], 30 July 1859, p. 2.
3. *Montreal Transcript*, 17 May 1860, p. 2.
4. I am indebted to Mr Edgar Andrew Collard and Professor John Bland for their generous counsel in ascertaining the nature of this scene.
5. J.R. Robertson, *The Diary of Mrs. John Graves Simcoe, Wife of the First Lieutenant-Governor of the Province of Upper Canada, 1792–6* (Toronto: The Ontario Publishing Co., Ltd., 1934), p. 97.
6. E.A. Collard, ''Grass on Beaver Hall Hill,'' *Montreal Gazette,* 31 Dec. 1982, p. B-2; K. Jenkins, *Montreal, Island City of the St. Lawrence* (Garden City, N.Y.: Doubleday & Company, Inc., 1966), pp. 218–219.
7. A. Kanof, *Jewish Ceremonial Art and Religious Observance* (New York: Harry N. Abrams, Inc., n.d.), pp. 84–93, 100–104.
8. *Dedication of the New Synagogue of Congregation Shaar Hashomayim* (Montreal: Eagle Publishing Co., Ltd., 1922), pp. 9–10.
9. *Jewish Chronicle* [London, Eng.], 15 Sept. 1865, p. 5.
10. *Montreal Gazette,* 16 Nov. 1866, p. 2.
11. *Journal de Québec*, 25 June 1862, p. 3; *Quebec Gazette,* 25 June 1862, p. 3.
12. Archives nationales du Québec, Montreal, Registers of Zion (Congregational) Church.
13. Culme, *Nineteenth-Century Silver,* pp. 194, 218.
14. M.G. Fales, *Early American Silver for the Cautious Collector* (New York: Funk & Wagnalls, 1970), pp. 52–53.
15. Poulin's mark is accompanied by pseudo-hallmarks which are like those sometimes found with the mark J.G.J in a rectangle, which is assigned to Judah G. Joseph of Toronto. Cf. Langdon, *Canadian Silversmiths* (1960), p. 126. It is not certain to whom they belong.
16. *Journal de Québec*, 17 July 1871, p. 1; 18 July 1871, p. 1; *Courrier du Canada* [Quebec], 17 July 1871, p. 2.
17. Swan, *Canada: Symbols of Sovereignty*, pp. 58, 61, passim; R.A. Pichette and A. Vachon, *An Exhibition of Armorial Silver from ''The Henry Birks Collection'' of Canadian Silver*, exhibition catalogue (Ottawa: The Heraldry Society of Canada, Public Archives of Canada, 1976), pp. 15–16.
18. He may be the same as William H. Tracey, who was active in Smiths Falls, Ontario, from 1857 until 1863. Cf. Burrows, *Canadian Clocks and Clockmakers*, pp. 128, 501.
19. *Ottawa Daily Free Press*, 4 July 1883, p. 3.
20. National Gallery of Canada, Curatorial Archives, Birks Ledger.
21. *Courrier du Canada* [Quebec], 8 Feb. 1895, p. 2; *Courrier de St-Hyacinthe*, 9 Feb. 1895, p. 2.
22. *Courrier du Canada* [Quebec], 27 Jan. 1896, p. 4.

Chapter V

1850–1899: Trophies and Sports Pieces

Trophies may be awarded for victories in many kinds of contests, though they are primarily associated with sports. This is true of all trophies in the Birks Collection dating from the second half of the nineteenth century, a period in which the popularity of this type of silver reached its peak. A few sports-related presentation pieces are also discussed in this chapter. All the pieces can be subdivided into convenient categories according to the type of sport for which they were awarded – be it snowshoeing, curling, or whatever. Only a few of these categories are represented in the Birks Collection, however, and not all examples of the categories to be found in the collection are treated here. Quality, as well as variety, has been a criterion in selecting the works to be discussed.

The history of competitive target shooting in Canada is closely allied to that of the militia and volunteer movement. The *Militia Act* of 1855 was destined to reorganize the militia by adding to it a new branch, the Active Volunteer Force. It was becoming recognized that Canada would have to assume an increasing share of its own defence, rather than rely on British garrisons. Accordingly, the new militia force was seen as providing a body of volunteers who would be properly trained and armed and who could be summoned at short notice. At first this force was envisaged as an adjunct to the British regular forces, to relieve them of matters of internal security. By the beginning of the 1860s that view had greatly altered. The British regulars were now seen as being supplementary to the militia in matters of defence; in other words, an increasing onus was being placed on the militia. The brunt of this situation was soon faced when the country was roused to a state of military alert because of the war in the United States. The end of the American Civil War did not do much to ease the situation, for by 1871 Britain had withdrawn all her garrisons from Canada and the Active Volunteer Force came to form the nucleus of the Canadian Army. A volunteer militia continued to perform a vital role in Canada's defence.

The rifle tournament was seen as a means of stimulating and maintaining interest in the volunteer movement, as well as ensuring a good supply of trained marksmen for the country's defence. Even after 1871 and through to the end of the century, rifle competitions were numerous and many trophies were awarded, both for the Canadian regulars (formed by the *Militia Act* of 1883) and the volunteer militia. However, the popularity of this type of competition peaked quite early, between 1862 and 1865.

In this light, it is not surprising to discover that the four most interesting shooting trophies in the Birks Collection date from the early 1860s, and three of these are associated with the volunteer movement. Several other shooting trophies in the collection are of later date. It must be added, moreover, that many of the more exceptional trophies were made toward the end of the century (cf. Fig. 28), and most of these are still in private collections.

The Nova Scotia Provincial Prize Cup, designed and executed by William Herman Newman[1] of Halifax, is one of the outstanding pieces of Nova Scotian silver from this period (Fig. 57). It was the grand prize at the Intercolonial Rifle Match held at Truro, Nova Scotia, from 10 to 12 September 1862. Competition was open to men and officers of the volunteers of the three Maritime provinces, and the cup was the gift of the government of Nova Scotia. The winner of the match was Major Pollard from Prince Edward Island. During the presentation address, Major-General Sir Charles Hastings Doyle, Commander of the British forces in the Atlantic area, aptly summarized the purpose of this and similar competitions: "The use of the rifle and these prize meetings are the keystone of the whole fabric of the volunteer movement, as I consider that, however useful the volunteer may be to his country, his services are of little avail unless he is acquainted with the use of the rifle...."[2]

The trophy is a standing cup with cover. An openwork calyx encases the lower cup proper, which is richly chased with ornament. At the front are the arms of Nova Scotia, flanked by flora native to the province

57

– mayflowers, Indian cups (pitcher plant), pigeon berries, and pickerelweed – revealing a concern for Naturalism. The shield with lion rampant at the centre of the arms is cast from gold mined in Nova Scotia. ''On the lid are very fine representations of a rifleman with his piece at the present, and a bugler at his side ready to sound the call.... The Nova Scotia Provincial Prize Cup is admitted on all hands to be very much superior to any similar work of art ever before manufactured in these Lower Provinces.''[3]

One of the truly great Canadian rifle tournaments of the nineteenth century was the Grand Rifle match held at Point St Charles, Montreal, which actually comprised twenty-two matches extending over a period of ten days, from 16 to 26 September 1863. Contestants came from both the regular military and volunteer forces in United Canada. Of the numerous prizes offered in competition announcements, some dozen and a half are silver cups and vases. The Field Officer's Cup, with the mark of Savage & Lyman, is one of these (Fig. 58). It was valued at $50, and if price is any indication, it would have been one of the more ordinary silver prizes. Two cups were valued at $200, the highest value, and another at $150. Notwithstanding, this prize cup, or rather tankard, is extremely handsome. It has a combination of chased and cast maple leaves on the back half of the body, a branchlike handle, and beaver finial. The moulded baseband has a narrow maple leaf frieze. In its naturalistic treatment, this tankard reveals references to other pieces of the period, such as those by Robert Hendery. It is to be noted that tankards were not a form generally made by Canadian silversmiths – that is, not until the later nineteenth century, and then almost always for use as trophies.

The Field Officer's Cup was competed for on 22 September 1863, and the match was ''open to all field officers of H[er]. M[ajesty].'s regular forces quartered in Canada, or of Canadian volunteer militia (excluding retired officers).''[4] The winner was Colonel Lord Alexander George Russell (1821–1907) of the Rifle Brigade (The Prince Consort's Own), who was then stationed in Hamilton. He won with a score of seven centres and three bull's-eyes in ten rounds, for a total of thirty-three points.[5]

Lord Russell was the tenth son of the sixth Duke of

Bedford, and brother of the Prime Minister, Lord John Russell. His was the life of a career soldier and he had a long-standing association with Canada. In 1847 he was appointed Aide-de-Camp to Lord Elgin, Governor-General of Canada (1847–1854). From 1862 to 1870 he was stationed in Canada with the First Batallion of the Rifle Brigade, which was under his command. From 1880 until 1889 he was Commander-in-Chief of Her Majesty's Forces in Canada.

The Griffin Cup (Fig. 59) is a militia trophy that comes from the West Coast, where the volunteer movement had also made considerable headway. This cup was made by Frederick R. Reichel (active c.1856–1867) of San Francisco, California, and was presented by James A. McCrea to the Victoria Volunteer Rifle Corps of Victoria for competition in the fall of 1864. Adverse weather prolonged the match by several days; Lieutenant and Adjutant James Gordon Vinter won it on 22 October, and not on 20 October as indicated by the inscription. The match was originally scheduled for the 20th, and the discrepancy would suggest that the inscription was already engraved on the cup before the competition was held and the name of the winner was added afterwards.

Sir Arthur Edward Kennedy, Governor of Vancouver Island, and his wife presided over the event. Mrs Kennedy awarded the prize and addressed the assembly with these words: "I feel certain that I express the sentiments of the ladies of this colony in wishing every success to a body of gentlemen who have undertaken the defence of our homes and the upholding of Her Majesty's honor in this distant land. The profession of arms, at all times honorable, is never more so than when voluntarily undertaken for a worthy purpose." In his reply, Vinter "expressed the honor he felt at being the winner of the first prize competed for on the Island."[6]

Vinter later became Captain in command of Company No. 2 of the Victoria Rifle Corps. After his death on 6 February 1879, the cup was put up for competition once again by the executor to Captain Vinter, Benjamin P. Griffin, hence the name of the cup. It was won on 18 October 1879 by Sergeant J.P. Kennedy, who in another contest on that same day won a place on the team to represent Canada at the next annual competition of the National Rifle Association of the United Kingdom at Wimbledon.[7]

From a design point of view, the Griffin Cup is a rather ordinary goblet. Nonetheless, it must have been specially ordered, as the ornament on the sides of the cup would suggest. Besides C-scrolls, ivy leaves, vine leaves, shamrocks, a thistle, and a rose, on each of two sides there is part of a flag with the Union Jack in the upper corner, which would seem to betoken a regimental flag (of the Victoria Rifle Corps?). Adjacent to the flag are a couple of spearheads and a trident.

Another goblet-form militia trophy, by Robert Hendery for Savage & Lyman (Fig. 60), was a prize at the annual Grand Rifle Match of the Quebec Rifle Association, which took place at the Beauport Flats near Quebec City, from 30 August to 5 September 1864. There were fourteen contests in all, and this goblet was the second prize for the first contest held on 30 August. Open to volunteers of Canada, this competition was won by Ensign James Esdaile of the Royal Light Infantry (of Montreal).[8] The cup of the goblet is an inverted bell form. The circular domed foot has chased spreading acanthus leaves and beaded edge, and four spinelike volutes extend from the foot up the stem. Such goblets are the most typical of sporting trophies in the later nineteenth century.

Trophies are also plentiful for winter sports, which were among the earliest organized in Canada. These sports included indigenous ones such as snowshoeing, or imported ones such as curling and skating. Snowshoeing as a recreational activity has a long history in Lower Canada. However, the first attempt at organization occurs with the Montreal Snow Shoe Club. Started in 1840, this club was formally organized in 1843. At that time, regular annual races were introduced, and shortly thereafter prizes for competition began to be awarded. Snowshoe clubs were soon founded in Quebec City and Ottawa, but Montreal remained the main centre for this sport and by the 1870s had a large number of clubs.

The earliest trophy in the Birks Collection comes from the Montreal Snow Shoe Club. It is a beaker made by Robert Hendery for Savage & Lyman (Fig. 61), and was presented to Nicholas Hughes for winning the fifth event in the M.S.S.C. annual races of 1857.[9] The *Montreal Gazette*, 14 March 1857 (p. 2), gives this description of the event: "Mile walk for $12 or a cup.

58

59

58 Field Officer's Cup, Grand Rifle Match, United Canada. Mark of Savage & Lyman, c.1863. Silver, gilt lined; 19.5 cm high. Birks (24005).

59 Griffin Cup, Victoria Volunteer Rifle Corps. Maker's mark of Frederick R. Reichel, San Francisco, c.1864. Silver, gilt lined; 20 cm high. Birks (24000).

60 Trophy, Quebec Rifle Association. Maker's mark of Robert Hendery for Savage & Lyman, c.1864. Silver; 18.5 cm high. Birks (27759).

61 Trophy, Montreal Snow Shoe Club. Maker's mark of Robert Hendery for Savage & Lyman, c.1857. Silver; 9 cm high. Birks (25147).

60

61

Mr. Hughes, Mr. H.H. Lamontagne, Mr. S.S. Macauley; and Indians Itachka and Moise. Mr. Hughes took the lead soon after starting, and came in the winner; but was closely pressed by Mr. Macauley...."

This beaker is an absolutely plain cylindrical form, except for the mouldings at the lip and base and the inscription. Nicholas Hughes, who was familiarly known as "Evergreen Hughes," was a founder and for many years either president or vice-president of the Montreal Snow Shoe Club, which later merged with the Montreal Lacrosse Club and the Montreal Bicycle Club to form the Montreal Amateur Athletic Association.

One of the most common types of goblet trophy is the 1872 Club Cup of the Alexandra Snow Shoe Club of Montreal (Fig. 62). With ovoid cup and low circular pedestal base, the stem of such trophies may consist of relevant pieces of sporting gear. In this instance these are snowshoes, in others hockey sticks, rifles, golf clubs, and so on. Many of these trophies were also fitted onto wooden pedestals, which was originally the case here. This trophy has marks of Savage, Lyman & Co. and the cruciform notched mark (see Fig. 89) of an unidentified workman believed to have been employed by Robert Hendery (also see Appendix I). It was won by J.J. Gilroy for the "Two Mile Club Race" at the Alexandra Snow Club annual races, 24 February 1872.[10]

Montrealers brought the sport of snowshoeing out west to Winnipeg. The Winnipeg Snow Shoe Club was founded in 1878 and the St George Snow Shoe Club in 1881. The latter was a branch of the Montreal club of the same name. The second Annual Cup of the Winnipeg Snow Shoe Club (Fig. 63), for the "Two Mile Race," was competed for on 20 March 1880 and won by Charles W. Radiger, a newcomer to Winnipeg and formerly a longtime member of the Montreal Snow Shoe Club.[11] This trophy bears the mark of Savage & Lyman.

Scots introduced their "roarin' game" of curling into Lower Canada toward the end of the eighteenth century. The Montreal Curling Club was the first club, and others were soon founded at Kingston (1820), Quebec City (1821), and Halifax (1825–26); by the 1850s the sport was quite widely dispersed – wherever the Scots settled. Curling was to retain a highly Scottish flavour

62

62 Club Cup for 1872 of the Alexandra Snow Shoe Club, Montreal. Attributed to Robert Hendery for Savage, Lyman & Co., c.1872. Silver, gilt lined; 17.5 cm high. Birks (25237).

63 Annual Cup for 1880 of the Winnipeg Snow Shoe Club. Mark of Savage & Lyman, c.1880. Silver, gilt lined; 15.1 cm high. Birks (25234).

63

for a long time to come.

In the nineteenth century, curling trophies were often referred to as tankards, whether or not they fitted the term. The Birks Collection does possess an actual curling tankard (Fig. 64), made by Robert Hendery & Co. for Gustavus Seifert (1831–1909) of Quebec City. The overall form is unusual and revives a seventeenth-century English type known as the peg-tankard, which is characterized by a drumlike shape, scroll handle, and flattish cushion lid almost flush with the sides of the drum. The Hendery tankard lacks the peglike markers on the inside that gave the prototype its name. The peg-tankard is associated with northeastern England, particularly York, from the 1660s through to the 1680s, and it is derived in turn from contemporary Scandinavian and Baltic models.

Historicism, like Naturalism, is a key constituent of the Victorian aesthetic, and fosters not only a study of historical styles for sources of inspiration but also encourages their revival. Stylistic modes of varying purity – some quite eclectic – result. Hendery reveals himself as being attuned to the general aspirations of this aesthetic – for example, in his use of Rococo ornament, or his accurate reproduction of an eighteenth-century American type, as in his porringer, figure 51. An earlier tankard (Fig. 58) has a form that is essentially eighteenth-century, but less obviously so, and the naturalistic ornament is contemporary Victorian. Similarly, the curling tankard is not a reproduction but an adaptation. To a seventeenth-century form he appends modern elements, such as a cast figure of a curler for a finial, and two small cast brooms on the lower handle terminal. On the front, an embossed and engraved wreath of thistles with beaver and maple leaves encircles the inscription: *Presented / to / Colonel T.L.J. Gallwey, / by the / STADACONA CURLING CLUB. / as a token of their high / esteem. / Quebec. 1868.*

From the dedication it may be inferred that this tankard is a presentation piece, rather than a trophy for some curling competition. The recipient was Colonel Thomas Lionel Gallwey, an Irishman, and officer in the Corps of Royal Engineers. Gallwey had an impressive career in the military. He was appointed Major-General in 1878, Lieutenant-General in 1882, Governor and Commander-in-Chief of Bermuda from

64 Gallwey Tankard, Stadacona Curling Club, Quebec City. Maker's mark of Robert Hendery & Co. for Gustavus Seifert, 1868. Silver; 17.7 cm high. Birks (25146).

65 Muir Tankard, Montreal Thistle Curling Club. Mark of Savage, Lyman & Co., c.1872. Silver parcel-gilt, and gilt lined; 27.2 cm high. Birks (24117).

66 Curling scene. Detail of Muir Tankard in Fig. 65.

1882 until 1888, and in 1895 Colonel Commandant of the Royal Engineers. During his early career he was stationed in Canada twice – in Montreal from 1849 until 1858, and in Quebec City from 1865 to 1868. Gallwey proved himself an avid curler while in Canada. During his first tour of duty he was a member of the Montreal Curling Club, and was a skip as well as club president just before leaving Canada in July 1858. To commemorate his departure he was presented with a silver claret jug by the members of three Montreal curling clubs – the Montreal, the Thistle, and the Caledonia. It is suspected that the Stadacona Club tankard was a presentation of like nature when he departed from Canada again ten years later.[12]

The Muir Tankard (Fig. 65) is a trophy of the Montreal Thistle Curling Club. Savage, Lyman & Co. was the retailer. This trophy is a flagonlike vessel sometimes known as a beer jug, and its main features are a cylindrical body, spreading foot, cast spout, handle, and a slightly domed and hinged cover. The basic form derives from seventeenth-century Germany, but it was fashionable in mid-Victorian England both for presentation pieces and trophies, and was usually overladen with a profusion of chased or repoussé ornament. In contrast with its models, the Muir Tankard is strikingly severe, with only a modicum of relief provided by such ancillary elements as the beaded edge of the foot, the silver-gilt curling stone finial, the two silver-gilt shieldlike plaques applied to the sides, and the engraving on the front – two thistle sprigs and a curling scene. The curling "stone" of the finial might properly be called a curling "iron." The large disc used in curling was customarily made of granite of a special type quarried in Scotland, and iron was widely used as a substitute in Quebec and eastern Ontario during the nineteenth century.

The engraved scene of a curling game on the front of the jug is a slightly free interpretation of a famous painting by the Scot, George Harvey, P.R.S.A., of 1835 (Fig. 66). Extremely popular with curling enthusiasts, the scene was frequently engraved, and is often found on curling trophies. For example, it appears in a reserve framed by thistles on the side of the Jubilee Trophy of the Montreal Curling Club (Fig. 24), and on the front of the Royal Caledonian Cup (also the Victoria Jubilee Trophy), which was given in 1897 by the Royal Caledo-

nian Curling Club (of Scotland) for competition among the clubs of the Canadian Branch of the R.C.C.C. The latter trophy also commemorates the Diamond Jubilee of Queen Victoria, which occurred the year it was donated.[13] The Harvey painting is described as follows: "On the right the minister, watched by the laird, has just thrown the penultimate stone which travels over the ice, amid the excited 'sooping up' of the other players to the end where the stones lie in a thick cluster."[14]

An inscription on one side of the Muir Tankard explains its purpose: *PRESENTED / to the / Montreal Thistle Curling Club, / BY / ROBERT MUIR, / to be played for annually by / THREE GAMES AT POINTS, / the player making the / Highest Aggregate Score / to be the / WINNER FOR THE YEAR, / and to be / FINALLY AWARDED / to whoever thus Wins / TWICE OUT OF / THREE SUCCESSIVE YEARS. / Montreal, / Jan.y 1872.* Robert Muir was for many years a member of the Montreal Thistle Curling Club, and was its president in 1858.[15] From another inscription we learn that the winners of this trophy were William Mulcaster Freer (1872), Edward B. Greenshields (1873), and James Esdaile (1874 and 1875). In accord with the terms of its presentation, the Muir Tankard became the property of Esdaile. He is presumably the same person who won the Quebec Rifle Association cup in 1864 (see Fig. 60).[16]

In the early sporting life of this country, equestrian sports were among the first for which silver prizes were awarded. Steeplechasing was adopted more slowly than regular horse racing, but by 1840 the Montreal Fox Hounds (also the Montreal Hunt) organized a steeplechase in Montreal, which is one of the earliest recorded. Others followed in that decade, and by the early 1850s the Montreal Fox Hounds held an annual steeplechase which was a great social occasion.[17] It is not certain when that organization began awarding trophies to winners, but the *Montreal Transcript* does relate on 21 October 1859 (p. 2) that the members of the Montreal Hunt had decided to go "to the trouble of getting out a silver cup, from England, in place of as heretofore having the purse in the shape of money." However, that same newspaper had reported the previous year, on 9 December 1858 (p. 2), that the Hunt Cup of the "Annual Steeple Chase of the Montreal

65

66

67 Hunt Cup for 1882 of the Montreal Fox Hounds. Maker's mark of Robert Hendery for J.R. Harper & Co., 1882. Silver, gilt lined; 40.3 cm high. Birks (24010).

68 Presentation cup, Province of Quebec Turf Club. Mark of J.R. Harper & Co., c.1882. Silver, gilt lined; 14.2 cm high. Birks (24119).

Hunt... was manufactured by Messrs. Hawksworth, Eyre & Co., Silversmiths, Platers and Electro-platers, of Sheffield.... The cup is a claret jug of the finest quality of electro-plate, elaborately embossed and ornamented with festoons of pine and grape." Hawksworth, Eyre & Co. also made the Hunt Cup for 1873, a highly wrought sculptural piece of "platinized sterling silver relieved with gold."[18]

From about 1858 onward, a silver trophy was awarded each year as the Hunt Cup, and it became one of the most coveted prizes for horse racing in the province of Quebec. Many of these cups were imported from Britain. The Hunt Cup for 1882 (Fig. 67) is in the Birks Collection, and it was made in Canada by Robert Hendery for J.R. Harper & Co. (James R. Harper, active c.1873–1888) of Montreal. Harper also supplied the Hunt Cup of 1885.[19] Of straightforward design, the cup features a simple bucket form supported on three crossed riding crops that rise from a circular pedestal. The bucket has straight sides tapering to a flat bottom, and two horseshoe-shaped handles that project obliquely upward from just under the rim. The front and back sides are engraved and chased with a wreath of maple leaves, the back framing a scene of a horse and rider jumping a hurdle, the front enclosing this inscription: *M·F·H· / HUNT CUP / Won by / M^r· A.M. Esdaile's / LITTLE JACK / also winner of the / GREEN & HUNTERS FLAT / 1882.*

"M.F.H." represents the Montreal Fox Hounds. It was about this time, 1882–83, that the name was officially changed to the Montreal Hunt, as it had already been popularly known for many years.[20] The Montreal Hunt Steeplechases for 1882 took place at the Blue Bonnets race course on 12 and 14 October. Because steeplechasing, as well as fox hunting, was very much a sport of gentlemen, this event was attended by many of the social elite of Montreal. The Hunt Cup had a value of $300, and these were the conditions of the competition:

> For horses that have been fairly and regularly hunted with the Montreal Hunt during the current year, and have not started for any race, except a Hunter's race, within twelve months, and *bona fide* the property of members of the Montreal Hunt on or before 15th September, 1882. To

be ridden by members elected on or before the same date, over about three miles of a fair hunting country. Weight, 12 stone. Entrance, $20.[21]

Mr Esdaile's "Little Jack" also won the Hunters' Flat and the Green Steeplechase. The latter was for horses that had never won a steeplechase or a hurdle race, and was open to members of any hunt club in Canada or the United States.[22]

Another equestrian cup in the Birks Collection is in the strict sense a presentation piece. Again with the mark of the retailer J.R. Harper & Co. of Montreal, it is presumably of Canadian make (Fig. 68). At least the sobriety of design speaks for its being Canadian. The cup is a tapered cylinder with two C-shaped handles. One side is quite plain except for a small perched sparrow hawk with inscribed ribbon-banner, engraved on the upper half – the crest and motto of Hugh Paton, the cup's recipient. The other side is almost covered with a decorative mantle in the form of a lengthy inscription, yet the polished surfaces shine through. It is these surfaces which, despite the dichotomy between front and back, provide cohesion to the overall form and enhance the integrity of the cup.

The inscription reads: *PROVINCE OF QUEBEC TURF CLUB / Presented to / HUGH PATON ESQ / HON^Y TREAS^R / BY THE STEWARDS AND OFFICERS / FOR THE YEAR 1882 / on RESIGNING the TREASURERSHIP / for / HIS LIBERALITY AND EXERTIONS IN / making the Meetings of the Club a success / JOSEPH HICKSON ESQ – ANDREW ALLAN ESQ. / Vice-Pres^{ts} / Capt. Campbell J.P. Dawes. / L^T COL. OUIMET DR CRAIK. / John Crawford E.T. Brooks. M.P. / JAS. O'BRIEN H.S. MACDOUGALL. / D. McEachran C.V. Temple. / E.A. WHITEHEAD. / STEWARDS / Duncan Robertson / SECT^Y.* The people named here were some of Montreal's most distinguished citizens. For example, Joseph Hickson was general manager of the Grand Trunk Railway, and Andrew Allan was president of the Montreal Ocean Steamship Company and president of the Merchant's Bank. Hugh Paton himself was president of the Sheddon Forwarding Co. Ltd.

One of the more remarkable equestrian meetings in western Canada was the 1886 Fall Meeting of the Manitoba Turf Club at Prairie Park in Winnipeg. In the

67

68

69 Road Race Cup of the Manitoba Turf Club. Maker's mark of Robert Hendery for W.S. Walker, c.1886. Silver, gilt lined; 29 cm high. Birks (27752).

70 Challenge Cup, Tecumseh Boat Club, London. Mark of J.G. Joseph & Co., c.1860. Silver; 19.9 cm high. Birks (25228).

71 Goblet. Maker's mark of Robert Hendery for Gustavus Seifert, c.1864. Silver; 20.8 cm high. Birks (25140).

Manitoba Free Press [Winnipeg], 22 September 1886 (p. 4), it was billed as "the largest race meeting ever held in Canada," with a total of sixteen different events over a period of four days. On 23 September, "Sleepy Jim," a horse owned by J.J. Johnstone, won the Road Race event for a prize of a silver cup valued at $250. The following is a summary of that event: "Sleepy Jim sold favorite in the race and his backers were not disappointed. If Blizzard had been in the race, however, there might have been a contest. As it was Jim had a very soft thing, winning as he pleased in any kind of time. Only three heats were necessary to decide the result."[23]

The trophy (Fig. 69) is a covered cup by Robert Hendery for W.S. Walker (active 1853–1892) of Montreal. In the character of some of its details, it recalls the earlier Hunt Cup, also by Hendery (Fig. 67). The pedestals of both are alike, with the same rinceaux frieze, which is repeated on the cover of the Road Race Cup. The stems are formed of three riding crops, and in the latter cup they are encircled by a laurel wreath. The front and back of the cups proper are engraved and chased with a foliate wreath.

The nineteenth century witnessed the organization of numerous other sports, and for many of them the awarding of silver trophies became customary after mid-century. Rowing and other aquatic sports were among these, and rowing regattas were documented from about 1810 and became widespread throughout Canada by the 1850s. In the late 1850s and 1860s, in particular, there was a sudden flourish of newly founded rowing and boat clubs in Upper Canada and elsewhere, and one of these was the Tecumseh Boat Club of London.[24] Among the first trophies offered by this club was the Challenge Cup (Fig. 70), with the mark of J.G. Joseph & Co., for pair-oared boat races that were part of the festivities in celebration of the Queen's Birthday, 24 May 1860. These races took place "at Westminster Bridge, starting from Hunt's mill-dam up the stream for about a mile." Six crews of three participated, with two crews in each race. A pair-oared sculling contest is engraved on the front of the cup below the inscription, where two sculls, each with three oarsmen, can be seen. The winning crew consisted of R. Labatt (stroke), C. Labatt (bow), and Bruce (cox). Engraved on the back of the cup are a pair of crossed oars, heraldically supported by the figure of an Indian and a bear and surmounted by a bear trippant. These are the arms of the Tecumseh Boat Club. The ropelike handles and edges of the cup and foot impart a nautical touch.[25]

Ice skating was another popular sport, and the mania for it really peaked about the 1860s. The establishment of the Quebec Skating Club was one of the first efforts at formal organization of the sport, and a goblet (Fig. 71) by Robert Hendery for Gustavus Seifert of Quebec City was presented to one of its early officers, engraved with this dedication: *PRESENTED TO / N.H. Bowen Esq! President. / By the Members of the / QUEBEC SKATING CLUB / in acknowledgement of the Valuable / Services rendered by him to the Club / during a period of Ten Years. / QUEBEC AUG! 1864.* This inscription is found on the cup in a reserve formed by two C-scrolls. A similar reserve on the opposite side contains the figure of a female skater, and on the sides are maple leaves. The foot of this goblet is similar to that of the Esdaile Cup by Robert Hendery for Savage & Lyman, which is of about the same date (see Fig. 60).

In its basic design, a billiard trophy by Robert Hendery & Co. (Fig. 72) is also of a type that is seen quite often – an earlier example is the Club Cup of the Alexandra Snow Shoe Club attributed to Robert Hendery (see Fig. 62). In this instance, three pieces of billiard equipment, a cue, bridge, and setting stick(?), replace the snowshoes of the stem. Four billiard balls are also placed on the flat top of the pedestal, and a laurel wreath, like that of the Road Race Cup of the Manitoba Turf Club by Robert Hendery (see Fig. 69), encircles the stem. Actually, the wreaths of the two cups were cast in the same mould. As evidenced here, Hendery frequently repeats identical or very similar decorative details on different pieces. An in-depth study of motifs from a large body of works might succeed in resolving whether or not Hendery was responsible for many pieces of silver that simply bear the marks of Savage & Lyman, or Savage, Lyman & Co.

In a reserve on one side of the cup is a scene with three figures around a billiard table, on the two flanking sides there are chased and engraved maple leaves, and in a reserve on the opposite side is this inscription: *Les Membres / DU / Cercle S! Denis / A LEUR / CHAMPION / 1866 / F.X. Beauchamp.*

69

70

71

WON BY
J. J. Johnstone's
"Sleepy Jim"
Time: 2.44½

72 Billiard trophy, Cercle St Denis, Montreal. Maker's mark of Robert Hendery & Co., c.1866. Silver, gilt lined; 19.4 cm high. Birks (27761).

73 Capital Lacrosse Club Cup, Ottawa. Maker's mark of Frederick Elkington of Elkington & Co., London, England, 1879–80 (cup proper); the cover, pennants and wreath are attributed to Hendery & Leslie. Silver, gilt lined; 48.3 cm high. Birks (25136).

72

73

A trophy for Canada's national game of lacrosse – the Capital Lacrosse Club Cup (Fig. 73) – was made under somewhat irregular circumstances. Below the rim of the bowl is the mark FE in a bilobate cartouche for Frederick Elkington of Elkington & Co. (a mark registered at the London, England, Assay Office on 24 May 1869), as well as London hallmarks for 1879–80. However, a long-standing tradition holds that parts of this trophy were completed by Hendery & Leslie – such as the maple leaf wreath and two pennants of the stem, and the cover and cast finial of a lacrosse player.[26] This opinion is borne out by both the design and the surface quality of the metal. Whereas the trophy proper has a brilliant if not sparkling surface, the cover and wreath are greyer and more subdued, yet richer. There is also an obvious discordance between the maple leaves of the cover and the remaining floral and foliate ornamentation of the bowl.

The trophy is inscribed thus: *PRESENTED TO / Sir A.P. Caron K.C.M.G. / POSTMASTER GENERAL / BY THE / Capital Lacrosse Club / CHAMPIONS / 1893.* The rationale behind this presentation is explained by the Ottawa *Citizen*, 22 December 1893 (p. 5): "The executive and players of the 'Capital Lacrosse Club' last evening showed their appreciation of the great services and good advice given them by their honorary president, Sir Adolphe Caron, Postmaster-General and patron of the national game, by presenting him with the magnificent trophy emblematic of the championship."

Notes

1. There is no mark on this piece but it is unquestionably by Newman, as the sources cited in note 3 below confirm.
2. *Morning Chronicle* [Halifax], 16 Sept. 1862, p. 2.
3. *Colonial Standard* [Pictou, N.S.], 16 Sept. 1862, p. 2; *Morning Chronicle* [Halifax], 9 Sept. 1862, p. 2; 13 Sept. 1862, p. 2; D.C. Mackay, *Silversmiths and Related Craftsmen of the Atlantic Provinces* (Halifax, N.S.: Petheric Press, 1973), pp. 73–74.
4. *Montreal Herald*, 16 Sept. 1863, p. 1.
5. *Montreal Transcript*, 15 Sept. 1863, p. 2; 23 Sept. 1863, p. 2; 6 Oct. 1863, p. 2; *Montreal Herald*, 23 Sept. 1863, p. 1; 6 Oct. 1863, p. 1; *Montreal Gazette*, 30 Sept. 1863, p. 2; 6 Oct. 1863, p. 2.
6. *The Daily British Colonist* [Victoria], 26 Oct. 1864, p. 3.
7. *The Daily British Colonist* [Victoria], 10 Oct. 1864, p. 3; 11 Oct. 1864, p. 3; 19 Oct. 1879, p. 3. Also J.K. Nesbitt, "Man about Town," *Daily Colonist* [Victoria], 15 July 1956, p. 5.
8. *Morning Chronicle* [Quebec], 26 Aug. 1864, p. 3; 31 Aug. 1864, p. 2; *Montreal Gazette*, 31 Aug. 1864, p. 2.
9. *Montreal Transcript*, 14 Mar. 1857, p. 2; H.W. Becket, *The Montreal Snow Shoe Club, Its History and Record* (Montreal: Becket Bros., 1882), p. 30.
10. *Montreal Herald,*, 26 Feb. 1872, p. 1; *Montreal Gazette*, 26 Feb. 1872, p. 2; Becket, *Montreal Snow Shoe Club*, p. 230.
11. *Winnipeg Daily Times*, 22 Mar. 1880, p. 4; Becket, *Montreal Snow Shoe Club*, p. 454.
12. *The Royal Montreal Curling Club*, pp. 27–28.
13. J. Kerr, *Curling in Canada and the United States: A Record of the Tour of the Scottish Team, 1902–3, and of the Game in the Dominion and the Republic* (Edinburgh: Geo. A. Morton, 1904), p. 146.
14. *National Gallery of Scotland Catalogue of Paintings and Sculpture* (Edinburgh: National Gallery of Scotland, 1957), p. 122. Also R.H. Hubbard et al., *Three Centuries of Scottish Painting*, exhibition catalogue (Ottawa: National Gallery of Canada, 1968), pp. 23, 52.
15. *The Montreal Thistle Curling Club 1843–1943* (Montreal: Privately Printed, 1943), pp. 28, 38.
16. *Montreal Gazette*, 15 Feb. 1872, p. 2; 21 Feb. 1873, p. 2; 20 Feb. 1875, p 3; *Montreal Herald*, 20 Feb. 1873, p. 1; 26 Feb. 1874, p. 2; 20 Feb. 1875, p. 2.
17. J.I. Cooper, *The History of the Montreal Hunt* (Montreal: The Montreal Hunt, 1953), pp. 16, 37; Lindsay, *Sport in Canada*, pp. 194, 203–204.
18. *Canadian Illustrated News* [Montreal], 7 June 1873, p. 356.
19. *Montreal Gazette*, 10 Oct. 1885, p. 8.
20. Cooper, *Montreal Hunt* (p. 58), says between 1881 and 1883.
21. *Montreal Gazette*, 16 Oct. 1882, p. 8.
22. *Montreal Gazette*, 13 Oct. 1882, p. 8; *Montreal Herald*, 11 Oct. 1882, p. 5; 13 Oct. 1882, p. 8; 16 Oct. 1882, p. 7.
23. *Daily Manitoban* [Winnipeg], 24 Sept. 1886, p.1; 23 Sept. 1886, p. 4; *Manitoba Daily Free Press* [Winnipeg], 23 Sept. 1886, p. 4.
24. Lindsay, *Sport in Canada*, pp. 165, 167; P. King, *Art and a Century of Canadian Rowing* (Toronto: Amberley House Limited [c.1980]), p. 15.
25. *London Free Press,* 7 May 1860, p. 3; 24 May 1860, p. 3; 26 May 1860, p. 3.
26. H. Ignatieff, "Canadian Presentation Pieces and Awards of Merit," *Canadian Collector*, XVI (Nov./Dec., 1981), p. 41.

Chapter VI

The Early Twentieth Century

The firm of Henry Birks & Sons Limited was in the forefront of silver production in the early part of the twentieth century, although there were other Canadian makers of some importance. The firm was founded in 1879 as a retail jeweller and silversmith under the name of Henry Birks & Co. In 1893 it became Henry Birks & Sons and, in 1905, Henry Birks & Sons Limited. It remained, however, a closed corporation. During the early years, Hendery & Leslie supplied most of its silver. A significant moment in the firm's history occurred on 17 February 1896 when an agreement was concluded with John Leslie whereby Birks would be the exclusive retailer for Hendery & Leslie in the Montreal area for all silver of a non-ecclesiastical nature. (Souvenir spoons formed a small exception to this agreement.) Hendery & Leslie was not restricted from supplying retailers elsewhere. Eventually, on 1 March 1899, the Hendery manufacturing concern was absorbed by Birks, which resulted in a transferral of designs, tools, and workmen. Thus Birks continued the older enterprise.

In contrast to Hendery & Leslie, Birks had a marketing strategy that aimed at serving the public directly instead of the wholesale trade. Consequently, to retain much of its predecessor's market, Birks was compelled to expand retail operations beyond Montreal. In 1901 Birks established a store in Ottawa. Others followed, and in a few years the firm had a network of stores across the country. Furthermore, in 1907 Birks took over the Montreal silver factory of the Gorham Co. of Canada. Before long, Birks was manufacturing and retailing a very large percentage of all presentation plate and trophies of Canadian make.

The earliest presentation piece of Birks make in the Birks Collection is a large oval tea tray with cast floral and foliate rim and two handles (Fig. 74). The flat bottom is richly engraved with ornament that encloses the following inscription: *PRESENTED TO / ROBERT ARCHER, ESQ. / ON THE OCCASION OF HIS MAR-RIAGE / 26THAPRIL, 1899. / BY HIS MONTREAL CO-DIRECTORS OF / THE BELL TELEPHONE COMPANY*

OF CANADA / CHARLES F. SISE. PRESIDENT. / ROBT MACKAY, VICE-PRESIDENT. / HUGH PATON. CHARLES CASSILS.

Strangely enough, the bride is not mentioned in the inscription. She was Henriette Glodie, daughter of Alfred Garneau and granddaughter of the historian François-Xavier Garneau. The marriage took place at the chapel of the Rideau Street Convent in Ottawa; and the *Ottawa Evening Journal* of 27 April 1899 (p. 3) provides a lengthy list of the wedding gifts, among which were numerous silver articles. At the end of that list is this mention of the tea tray: "The president and directors of the Bell Telephone Company, Montreal, sent the design of a lovely silver salver, which owing to the exquisite work upon it will not be ready until the summer." Thus, the tray was actually given some months after the date recorded in the inscription – or possibly even later (see Appendix I).

A three-handled cup (Fig. 75) can be precisely dated from the identifying marks for 1905 of the Birks workman John J. Walsh (see Fig. 98); 1905 is also the year given by the inscription. This type of cup is common enough at the time.[1] It has three harp-shaped handles of staghorn, each with a large silver boss at its uppermost angle. The dedication on the front of the bowl reads: *PRESENTED / TO / Dr. Thos C. Brainerd / BY HIS FELLOW MEMBERS OF THE / SHAWINIGAN CLUB / In remembrance of his long services as Treasurer / Montreal 1st May 1905.*

Of about the same date is a horse's hoof mounted in silver, complete with a thin silver horseshoe, by Henry Birks & Sons (Fig. 76). The custom of creating pieces of this kind originated in England, where it had currency in the second half of the nineteenth century: the lower portion of one or more of the hooves of a champion steed was removed after its death, and then mounted in silver as a keepsake for the owner or, as in this case, for the jockey. Usually the hoof was converted into a snuffbox; here it is an inkwell. The following inscription is engraved on the circular lid: *MOONSTONE / winner of / Montreal Hunt Cup*

74

75

76

Steeplechase / 1880 / Ridden by / Mʳ. J.A.L. Strathy.
James Alexander Lawrason Strathy was a well-known Montreal equestrian who won the Montreal Hunt Cup Steeplechase in 1880, 1881, and 1886. He was also a partner in the brokerage firm of Gordon Strathy & Company and an organizer of the Montreal Trust & Deposit Company.

A communion service by Birks (Fig. 77) also warrants consideration, although it is not within the scope of this study in the strict sense as it is an item of church plate. The justification for including it here is partly that it is the only plate in the Birks Collection that is definitely known to have been given to a church by a private donor and was not acquired by the church itself. In addition, the gift has a special and highly personal significance, as revealed by the dedication on the flagon: *TO THE / Glory of God / AND IN LOVING MEMORY OF / Rt. Rev. James Carmichael D.D., D.C.U. / FOURTH BISHOP OF MONTREAL, / AND HIS DEVOTED WIFE / Emma Du Bourdieu, / PRESENTED BY / THEIR AFFECTIONATE SONS TO / The Bishop Carmichael Memorial Church, / EASTER 1911.*

A native of Ireland, Bishop Carmichael was Anglican Bishop of Montreal from 1906 until his death in 1908. He had two sons, the Reverend James Saumarez Carmichael, also an Anglican clergyman, and Frederick Carmichael, a banker. In 1911 the newly constructed Church of St Alban's in Montreal was dedicated as the Bishop Carmichael Memorial Church, and that same year Carmichael's sons presented the communion service to the church.[2] From a stylistic point of view, the service is essentially Gothic Revival, although only in its basic forms, as ornament here is nearly totally absent. This service is in fact a stock Birks catalogue item of the time.[3]

Certainly one of the most curious pieces from this period is a punch bowl by Birks dated 1910/15 (Fig. 78). The exact history of this piece is obscure, but evidently it was commissioned for the Connecticut Valley Poultry Association (of Vermont) as an annual award, along with a cash prize of $500, for the outstanding chicken flock (or rooster?) in the region. The partially scalloped rim of the bowl calls to mind a monteith; and indeed it would seem to have served as a receptacle for punch, or some other beverage.

77

75 Three-handled cup. Maker's mark of John J. Walsh as workman for Henry Birks & Sons, 1905. Silver, horn (handles); 26.4 cm long. Birks (25242).

76 Inkwell. Maker's mark of Henry Birks & Sons, c.1905–10. Silver, hoof (equine); 15.5 cm long. Birks (25244).

77 Communion service (chalice, flagon, paten, and credence paten with cover). Maker's mark of Henry Birks & Sons (c.1911), except for small paten (French, 19th century). Silver; 28 cm high (flagon). Birks (24032, 27763, 24148, 27764).

78

Chicken motifs predominate rather obtrusively, as in the handles which are shaped like chickens, the four legs with outspread claws which support the bowl, and the engraved scene of the inside of a chicken coop which is enclosed in a shaped reserve on the side of the bowl. Even the plump, oblong shape of the bowl bears similarities to the body of a chicken. To these motifs are added Classical ornament consisting of acanthus leaves, rosettes, a laurel border on the rim, imbrication, and Rococo C-scrolls. Extraordinarily enough, the acanthus leaves and imbrication convey an almost featherlike quality. Also quite incongruously, a small coat-of-arms of Montreal with motto *CONCORDIA SALUS* is affixed to the rim where it peaks at front and back. The whole comprises a rather bizarre assemblage of decorative elements and no doubt was custom-designed.

Of two relevant items in the collection for this period by silversmiths other than Birks, one is a trowel (Fig. 79) with the mark of Andrew & Co., Ltd. (George Andrew and Charles Norman Andrew, active c.1901/05–1930) of Winnipeg. It is not certain whether Andrew is the maker, although that may be the case as it was a firm of manufacturing jewellers. George Andrew, the founder of the firm, started business in Winnipeg in 1875. By 1892 it became Andrew & Co., and sometime between 1901 and 1905 Andrew & Co., Ltd.[4] The handle of the trowel is of ivory, carved in the form of the upper torso and head of a male figure. The upper blade is engraved with maple leaves, the lower blade with this inscription: *PRESENTED / TO / Alex Haggart Esq. / Vice Chairman / OF THE / WINNIPEG PUBLIC SCHOOL BOARD / on the / occasion of laying the corner stone / OF THE / Lord Selkirk / School / Sept.! 5!.b / 1908.* Haggart was elected to Parliament from Winnipeg in 1908 and 1911.[5]

Toronto was another silver production centre at this time, and the Birks Collection has a two-handled cup with cover (Fig. 80) by Roden Bros., Ltd. (active c.1915–1953) of that city. Reproducing a popular late eighteenth-century English type, the cup is not just a revival or adaptation of an older design, but exhibits a correctness that belies servile imitation (cf. Fig. 1). This mimetic aspect characterizes many twentieth-century trophies, which so often emulate eighteenth-century English models.

79

80

78 Punch bowl. Maker's mark of Henry Birks & Sons, c.1910–15. Silver, gilt lined; 48.5 cm long. Birks (24121).

79 Trowel with ivory handle. Mark of Andrew & Co., Ltd., c.1908. Silver; 26.3 cm long. Birks (25145).

80 Two-handled covered cup. Maker's mark of Roden Bros., Ltd., c.1915-50. Silver gilt, wood (pedestal); 34.5 cm high. Birks (25246).

81 Trophy, Canadian National Horse Show. Maker's mark of Frank T. Proctor, c.1907. Silver; 15.2 cm high. Royal Ontario Museum (980.103.2).

81

The cup here is a replica of the Connaught Cup, first presented to the Ontario Jockey Club in 1912 for annual competition by Field Marshall HRH The Duke of Connaught and Strathearn, who was Governor-General of Canada from 1911 to 1916. The Connaught Cup has hallmarks for 1911–12 and the maker's mark of Sebastian Henry Garrard for Garrard's of London. For many years, replicas of this cup were presented to the various winners, and the more recent ones were made by Birks. Many earlier examples were made by Roden, which may explain the cup in the Birks Collection, although it was never actually used for presentation purposes. Apparently this replica was transferred to the Birks Collection in about 1957 when Birks absorbed the Roden firm.

Certainly there are many trophies of this period that are not reproductions, and some of these begin to demonstrate novel conceptions for a new century. Such is a two-handled cup (Fig. 81) by Frank T. Proctor (active c.1891–1931) of Toronto, which is at the Royal Ontario Museum. One side of the cup is inscribed: *CANADIAN NATIONAL HORSE SHOW / 1907 / FIRST;* and the other side: *POLO PONIES / K·R· MARSHALL.* There is a lingering historicism here – for example, in the ubiquitous bowl form, which has an air of the Antique about it. The scrolled harp-handles, of eighteenth-century type, are almost inappropriate. Likewise, the frieze that embraces the rim of the cup recalls Classical Greek relief sculpture, or more properly its Neo-Attic derivative. The frieze is not continuous but broken up into a series of metope-like panels, and these consist of a sequence of two small panels and one large one, repeated regularly. The low relief, the silhouetting of relatively simple forms against a plain background, and the overall clarity of execution all convey a "Neo-Attic" aspect. From another standpoint, the individual equine scenes are contemporary. Even if the piece is still rooted in a traditional framework, the overall impression is of a striving for innovation and a tendency to modernity within the bounds of a pastiche. The design definitely has no parallel in Canada up to this time.

Tastes were decidedly changing in Canada at the beginning of the twentieth century, and this is reflected in the fashion for silver presentation pieces and trophies, which declines greatly as the century advances. We must conclude that this type of plate belongs, above all, to the second half of the nineteenth century. In keeping with their intended purpose, presentation pieces succeed in commemorating for posterity many personal and public events and accomplishments, both great and small, and thereby enhance our understanding of what our ancestors esteemed in their lives. The Henry Birks Collection of Canadian Silver preserves the largest body of early Canadian presentation silver to be found in a museum. The opportunity afforded by its study not only reveals much about the character of Canadian silver in this period, but also allows some fascinating insights into Canadian social history.

Notes

1. For an almost identical cup, see *The Royal Montreal Curling Club 1807–1932* (Montreal: Privately Printed, 1932), p. 46.
2. *Montreal Gazette*, 23 Sept. 1911, p. 2.
3. For example, see Henry Birks & Sons, Ltd., catalogue for 1913, p. 114.
4. *Manitoba Free Press* [Winnipeg], 11 July 1907, p. 19; 25 Nov. 1915, p. 3.
5. *Manitoba Free Press* [Winnipeg], 7 Sept. 1908, p. 12.

Appendices

Appendix I   Some Notes on Silversmiths' Marks

In nineteenth-century Canada there was no officially regulated marking system for silver. This fact, plus an increased complexity in the relationships of various sectors of silversmithing (as discussed in Chapter III), has created problems in the study of marks. Large numbers of marks on Canadian silver, particularly beginning with the second quarter of the century, have yet to be properly documented and sorted out. A comparable, if less grievous situation exists in the United States and even in Britain, where the introduction of the *United Kingdom Customs Act* of 1842 allowed not only working silversmiths but also retailers and importers to register makers' marks.[1] In sum: identification of the owner of a so-called maker's mark does not necessarily reveal the maker.

A maker's mark traditionally consisted of a silversmith's initials, to which a device might be added. In the nineteenth century, marks sometimes assumed the additional form of a last or even full name. By the second quarter of the century, these lettered "makers'" marks often came to signify a retailer instead of a maker. The situation was aggravated as production became concentrated in fewer workshops, while retailers multiplied.

Pseudo-hallmarks, which imitated British hallmarks, were also introduced in the early nineteenth century. Initially these were intended to serve as quality marks, or as a type of warranty comparable to that of hallmarks on imported British silver; and no doubt the public even accepted them as such, although they were quite unofficial. However, it was not long before these pseudo-hallmarks developed an additional significance, particularly for the makers to the trade who required some new means of identifying their products other than by the traditional lettered marks, which were being taken up by retailers as well. The result was that pseudo-hallmarks often came to function as trademarks. They were applied to a product by a maker, and then a dealer would appose his own lettered mark. Unavoidably, variables are encountered in a marking system that is not official, and sometimes pseudo-hallmarks on a piece can also belong to a dealer, or all marks belong to a maker. In the latter case they often signify a dual role of both silversmith and retailer, or manufacturing retailer.

The intention here is to present some thoughts that derive directly from the study of presentation silver – particularly pieces in the Birks Collection – as a preliminary step in resolving some unknowns about nineteenth-century marks. (Note that all the works discussed are not necessarily treated in the main text of this book.) The nature of the presentation silver in the Birks Collection has determined the focus of our study. The two main groups of marks to be examined are those of the Savage and the Hendery firms: there are not enough pieces associated with the other firms to warrant treatment here.

The positive identification of marks – and the establishment of any form of chronology for their use – depends on the availability of primary documentation. In any study of Canadian marks, particularly marks of Quebec silversmiths, the principal source of documented pieces is ecclesiastical plate and church records. Unfortunately, such an approach has no application for the Savage firms, as they were engaged exclusively in a secular trade. The situation is not entirely dissimilar for Hendery, as most of his ecclesiastical plate dates from the later years of his career. On the other hand, and this is due in part to the relative abundance of material, it has been recognized that presentation silver offers an alternative source of datable pieces, especially for the Savage and Hendery firms which were so deeply involved in this aspect of the trade.

To ensure as accurate a data base as possible, several steps were followed in evaluating material for this study. It scarcely need be said that inscriptions in themselves can be rather tenuous and on occasion even hazardous as a means of dating a piece. However, presentation pieces frequently have the advantage of being recorded in newspapers or elsewhere, often enabling the verification of an inscribed date. That in itself is still not quite sufficient, for it does not guarantee when an object was actually made. A further criterion has therefore been used and that is whether or not a piece gives sufficient indication of having been custom-made for the occasion. If there is visual evidence that it has (i.e., in the uniqueness of design), and the documentation is in accord with the inscription, then the date is accepted as such. Otherwise, if the piece is thought to be a stock item, the date is indicated as being approximate.

By this means, a number of documented reference points have been established, enabling a chronological framework to be sketched out. This framework is to be regarded as strictly provisional: actually many more objects must be examined in a similar manner before a rigid schema can be developed. The information presented merely amounts to a first step toward such a schema.

It is also to be pointed out that not all of the observations recorded here are entirely original. Many have been made by Louis Carrier, Harry Allice, John E. Langdon, and Helena Ignatieff, among others. These ideas have now been amplified, drawing on presentation silver as a dating tool, and are published here for the first time.

In the notes that ensue, the term "mark" signifies a so-called maker's mark or lettered mark. Pseudo-hallmarks are in the form of symbols – for example, a lion passant. As indicated earlier, most of the pieces referred to are in the Birks Collection, although a few in other collections are also noted. The many general comments reflect a summation of personal observations made over a number of years.

Marks of the Savage Firms

Some uncertainty persists about the earliest Savage marks. John E. Langdon has ascribed an impressed mark with relief letters GS in a sunken rectangular frame (enclosure) to George Savage Sr (1767–1845).[2] Although that attribution has yet to be substantiated, at present one can state that it is certainly a rare enough mark, and therefore under any circumstances it can be assumed that it was little used. Another mark also

sometimes given to the senior Savage is GS incuse (i.e., with sunken letters), occasionally with a period after either letter. That mark actually belongs to the later Gustavus Seifert of Quebec City (cf. Fig. 96).

The two marks most readily associated with George Savage & Son are GS&S and G.SAVAGE&SON (each in a rectangular frame), which are possibly the most common Canadian silver marks in the second quarter of the century. Illustrated in figures 82 and 83, either or both marks must have been introduced by 1828, or possibly earlier. At least the GS&S mark was in use by 1830 at the latest, for it is also known with pseudo-hallmarks of Salomon Marion who died that year.[3] Until the dates of the Savage partnership are more firmly established, further speculation remains pointless. The pseudo-hallmarks accompanying the examples given are those of Peter Bohle (1786–1862) as silversmith.

Figure 84 shows Bohle's mark PB in a rectangle along with the same sovereign's head as in figures 82 and 83, and a different lion passant gardant sinister. Together, these three pseudo-hallmarks (the two here and the lion passant above) are among a number that belonged to Bohle. It is true that the outer edges of the frame of the sovereign's head now show some irregularities, but here these are symptomatic of a wearing puncheon and not a new one, and hence reflect a later date. Whereas this sovereign's head occurs occasionally in conjunction with marks of George Savage & Son – that is, with the two above – the second lion passant does not, and it apparently postdates these marks. Moreover, the use of these two pseudo-hallmarks together (again, as in figure 84) is not known with marks of Bohle & Hendery, or for that matter on any piece of silver datable to the 1850s, and therefore must predate that partnership, which began c.1851. This combination of circumstances would place the use of these two pseudo-hallmarks conjointly to the 1840s. The same lion passant continues to appear later on Savage & Lyman silver (see below).

The mark SAVAGE in a rectangle also occurs fairly frequently with the two preceding pseudo-hallmarks, as in figure 85. In fact, the first appearance of these two pseudo-hallmarks together coincides approximately with the appearance of the SAVAGE mark. The introduction of the SAVAGE mark may or may not

82

83

84

85

82 Marks on tablespoon by Peter Bohle for George Savage & Son, c.1825–42. Birks (25870).

83 Marks on dessert fork by Peter Bohle for George Savage & Son, c.1825–42. Birks (25853.8).

84 Marks on mug (Fig. 9) by Peter Bohle, c.1840–50. Birks (24086).

85 Marks on mug (Fig. 10) by Peter Bohle for George Savage & Son, c.1840–50. Birks (25204).

86 Marks on claret jug (Fig. 32) by Robert Hendery for Savage & Lyman, c.1859. Birks (27754).

87 Marks on Annual Cup for 1880 of the Winnipeg Snow Shoe Club (Fig. 63) retailed by Savage & Lyman, c.1880. Birks (25234).

88 Marks on fish slice (Fig. 43) retailed by Savage & Lyman, c.1866. Birks (25967).

89 Marks on Club Cup of the Alexandra Snow Shoe Club (Fig. 62) attributed to Robert Hendery for Savage, Lyman & Co., c.1872. Birks (25237).

follow immediately upon the cessation of the business association of George Savage Sr with his son Joseph. Nevertheless, this mark succeeds those commonly associated with their partnership, although there may have been a period, for example in the early 1840s(?), when the use of all these marks actually overlapped. Thus, SAVAGE in a rectangle was apparently the only mark used by George Savage & Son in the last years of the firm, until 1851. It is not the mark of George Savage Sr as it has often been attributed.[4] Unlike the earlier firm marks, this mark is not found with the same variety of pseudo-hallmarks, suggesting that fewer silversmiths were now supplying Savage. In fact, the above pseudo-hallmarks of Bohle occur with such frequency as to imply that he was the principal supplier at this time, which actually accords with tradition.[5]

The SAVAGE mark also continues to be used in the 1850s by Savage & Lyman, and present evidence seems to indicate that it may have been the only mark used during the early years of that firm. This mark occurs on the following presentation pieces (National Gallery accession numbers for the Birks Collection in parentheses): a tea and coffee service (24122–24125) of 1851 by Bohle & Hendery (see Fig. 91), a beaker (25147) of c.1857, and two goblets (27755, 27756) of c.1859 by Robert Hendery.

Toward the end of the 1850s, Savage & Lyman began to introduce other marks, which take on a number of variant forms. The earliest datable one in the Birks Collection is on the claret jug (27754) by Robert Hendery (Fig. 86), which was presented in January 1859, although the jug may have been made sometime before that. Adoption of other marks about this time, as well as the discontinuance of the mark SAVAGE in a rectangle, may have been occasioned, at least in part, by the death of Joseph Savage in February 1859. Among the new marks are:

(Note: In f), and in subsequent references to marks, the diagonal symbol indicates that the mark appears on two lines.)

a) SAVAGE & LYMAN (each framed)
b) SAVAGE&LYMAN (in rectangular frame)
c) S&L (in rectangular frame)
d) S.L. (incuse)
e) SAVAGE&LYMAN (incuse)
f) SAVAGE / &.LYMAN (incuse)

Also see Langdon, *Guide to Marks*, pp. 74–75.

Most of the above marks were used by the firm until about 1868, when it became Savage, Lyman & Co. However, as suggested by the examples given here, mark f) may perhaps have been retained up until the beginning of the 1870s. That mark is on these pieces by Robert Hendery: water pitcher, six goblets, and tray (26097–26104) of 1859 (see Fig. 93), pitcher (25135) of 1860, child's cup (25208) of c.1860, pitcher (25139) of 1861, goblet (27759) of c.1864, child's cup (25236) of c.1866, claret jug (acc. no. 961.170) of c.1859 and a goblet (acc. no. 962.1) of c.1871, the latter two at the Royal Ontario Museum. Mark a) is on the Regiment Cup (25239) of c.1868, on a child's cup (acc. no. 964.85.1) of c.1868 at the Royal Ontario Museum, and on the Annual Cup of the Winnipeg Snow Shoe Club (25234) of c.1880 (Fig. 87). The latter example indicates that at least mark a), if not others (?), was revived when the firm again reverted to the name of Savage & Lyman from 1878 until 1885. Mark b) is on the Field Officer's Cup (24005) of c.1863, a mug (25209) of c.1864, and on the pair of fish carvers (25967, 25968) of c.1866 (Fig. 88). Mark e) is on these pieces by Hendery: goblet (24138) of c.1859, claret jug (27754) of c.1859 (Fig. 86), and a beaker (27757) of c.1860–1865.

While the pseudo-hallmarks that accompany the above retailers' marks of Savage & Lyman generally can be identified with Robert Hendery as maker, there are a couple of pairs that form an exception. As these particular pseudo-hallmarks are exclusive to silver with Savage marks, it is not certain whether they are special makers' marks or simply additional marks of the retailer. The pair illustrated in figure 88 is found on the Field Officer's Cup (24005) of c.1863, a mug (25209) of c.1864, and the pair of fish carvers (25967, 25968) of c.1866. The other pair of pseudo-hallmarks is found on the Regiment Cup (25239) of c.1868, and a child's cup (acc. no. 964.85.1) of c.1868 at the Royal Ontario Museum. As indicated in figures 87 and 89, this second pair continued to be used with the marks of Savage, Lyman & Co., as well as by the later Savage & Lyman firm, up until the early 1880s.

86

87

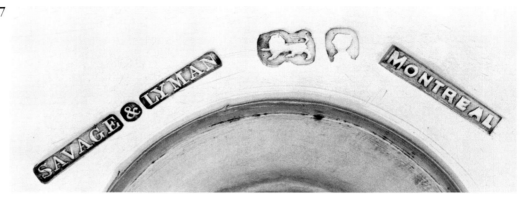

89

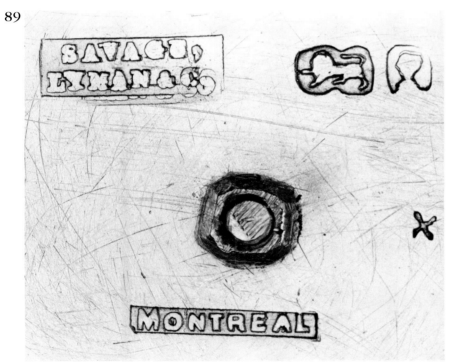

88

90 Marks on fork by Bohle & Hendery, c.1851–56. Birks (26429.2).

91 Marks on coffee pot (Figs. 20, 22) by Bohle & Hendery for Savage & Lyman, 1851. Birks (24125).

92 Marks on dessert spoon by Bohle & Hendery, c.1851–56. Birks (26427).

93 Marks on tray (Fig. 33) by Robert Hendery for Savage & Lyman, 1859. Birks (26104).

94 Marks on mug by Robert Hendery, c.1860–65. Birks (25198).

For the period of Savage, Lyman & Co. (1868–1878), different distinguishing marks were in use, and among these were:

a) SAVAGE, / LYMAN&CO (in rectangular frame)
b) SAVAGE. / LYMAN&Cº (in rectangular frame)
c) SAVAGE / LYMAN&CO (incuse)
d) SL&Cº (in rectangular frame)

Also see Langdon, *Guide to Marks*, p. 75.

Mark a) is on a butter dish (25309) of c.1869, on the Muir Tankard (24117) of c. 1872, on the Club Cup of the Alexandra Snow Shoe Club (25237) of c.1872 (see Fig. 89), and on a mug at the Royal Ontario Museum (acc. no. 977.215.3) of c.1870. Mark c) is found on a child's cup (24142) of c.1877 by Robert Hendery.

Marks of the Hendery Firms

At present, no marks of any kind can be directly associated with the early career of Robert Hendery – that is, before 1850.[6] The earliest known are those shared in partnership with Peter Bohle, lasting from c.1851 to 1856, which include one lettered mark PB / & / RH in a rectangle, used almost exclusively for flatware. Generally their hollow ware was struck with two of several different pseudo-hallmarks (the range of pseudo-hallmarks was greater for flatware); these include a lion passant gardant sinister and a sovereign's head dexter, as appear on a fork with the above lettered mark in figure 90 (also note the leopard's head), as well as on the tea and coffee service (24122–24125) of 1851 with the mark of Savage (Fig. 91). Bohle & Hendery had another similar lion passant puncheon, which is that used earlier by Bohle (cf. Fig. 84), and a variant of the preceding sovereign's head, which in fact derives from the same puncheon and has merely developed a wedge-shaped boss at the upper extremity. It is in this second form that the sovereign's head is most commonly known. This second pair of pseudo-hallmarks is illustrated with the mark of the partners in figure 92.

Evidently these pseudo-hallmarks were interchanged – that is, the two variant impressions of the sovereign's head with the two lions passant – though their usual disposition is as in the two pairs treated above (Figs. 91 and 92). The sovereign's head of the first pair is also sometimes found with the lion passant of the second; but only rarely is the sovereign's head of the second found with the lion passant of the first. Was the first lion passant discontinued sometime during the course of the partnership? Upon the dissolution of Bohle & Hendery, the latter partner would seem to have succeeded to the other two puncheons (the sovereign's head having received the upper boss before this time), and carried on using them as his own.

That these two puncheons belonged to Hendery in the late 1850s is attested to by the pseudo-hallmarks present together with his mark R.HENDERY incuse on a presentation pitcher at the Royal Ontario Museum (acc. no. 972.60.60) of 1859. Contemporary newspaper reports also record Hendery as the maker of that piece.[7] This same combination of mark and pseudo-hallmarks can be found on a holy water stoup at the Montreal Museum of Fine Arts (acc. no. 952.Ds.21) and on flatware in the Birks Collection. Evidently Hendery used these pseudo-hallmarks as late as 1860. They are on the following presentation pieces by him: beaker (25147) of c.1857, water pitcher, six goblets, and tray (26097–26104) of 1859 (Fig. 93), a claret jug at the Royal Ontario Museum (acc. no. 961.170) of c.1859, two goblets (27755, 27756) of c.1859, goblet (24138) of c.1859, pitcher (25135) of 1860, and a child's cup (25208) of c.1860.

Hendery also adopted another pair of more distinctive pseudo-hallmarks sometime after about 1856, and they have the form of a lion rampant sinister in an oval and a sovereign's head dexter in a square with clipped corners (Figs. 94 and 95). These pseudo-hallmarks are struck on a pitcher (25139) of 1861, the earliest that can be dated among other pieces in the Birks Collection. They are also found frequently enough in conjunction with the mark SAVAGE in a rectangle on flatware to suggest a couple of years of overlap in their use – for example, c.1857 to 1859. Aside from serving as identity marks, they offer little as a dating tool in themselves, except in very general terms, as they were the most commonly used by Hendery, and by Hendery & Leslie; in addition, an almost indistinguishable variant of the lion rampant and the sovereign's head continued to be used by Henry Birks & Sons for Roman Catholic Church plate right up until about 1925.

90

91

92

94

93

Another pair of pseudo-hallmarks attributed to Robert Hendery can be seen in figure 86. Found on the jug (27754) of the claret set of c.1859 (see Fig. 32), this attribution depends on the two companion goblets, which have the earlier pseudo-hallmarks of Hendery, as in figure 93, and which there is little reason to doubt were by the same maker. There is also a claret jug of very similar design at the Royal Ontario Museum (acc. no. 961.170) of c. 1859, which has the earlier Hendery pseudo-hallmarks. The pseudo-hallmarks on the jug in the Birks Collection are small, and hence are more usual to flatware or small items; for example, they can be found on a beaker (27757).

Toward the late 1850s, Hendery would also seem to have begun adopting marks consisting of his name or initials. They take several forms:

a) R.HENDERY (incuse)
b) R.H. (incuse)
c) RH (incuse)
d) RH (in rectangular frame)
e) R.H (in shaped frame)

Also see Langdon, *Guide to Marks*, pp. 36–37.

Mark a) is the only one encountered on presentation silver in the Birks Collection. It can be dated as early as 1859 on the basis of a presentation pitcher at the Royal Ontario Museum (acc. no. 972.60.60), referred to above. Unlike the disposition of marks on the pitcher, this mark is usually accompanied by Hendery's lion rampant and its companion sovereign's head (cf. Fig. 94), as in the following pieces: porringer (25050) of c.1863, goblet (25229) of c.1863, and two goblets (27118, 27119) of c.1864.

Apparently mark a) continued to be used during the period of Robert Hendery & Co. (c.1866–1870), when the letters ''& Co'' were merely appended to it, as in figure 95. It is in this form on the following: goblet (27761) of c.1866, goblet (25232) of c.1866, tray (24126) of c.1867, and two kiddush goblets (24137, 25134) of c.1869.

Along with each of the preceding are Hendery's lion rampant and sovereign's head. After about 1870 they became not just his chief but almost exclusive identity marks, which is not at all untoward for it was about this time that he withdrew from retail activities to con-

centrate wholly on the manufacturing and wholesale end of things. From here on these pseudo-hallmarks are often found adjacent to the mark (initials or full name) of a retailer; an early example of about 1864 is illustrated in figure 96, which has the incuse G.S mark of Gustavus Seifert (1831–1909) of Quebec City.[8]

A couple of other noteworthy marks were introduced later on by the firm of Hendery & Leslie (1887–1899). These new marks are, both incuse, HENDERY & LESLIE and H&L.

Marks of Henry Birks & Sons

For information on the earliest Birks marks – for example, those of Henry Birks & Co. – the reader should consult the various publications of John E. Langdon. The intent here is simply to present two tables outlining the basic marking system of Henry Birks & Sons Limited, with whose kind permission they are reproduced.

Table 1 (p. 102), which has never before been published, shows the marks of various workmen (silversmiths) who were employed in the Birks silver factory during the early part of this century. The upper section of this table lists marks in the form of letters, the lower section various symbols in the form of notches and dots. The use of notches as a means of identifying particular workmen is of English origin and a particularly nineteenth-century practice, essentially for flatware but also for hollow ware in such cities as Birmingham and Sheffield.[9] Hendery implemented a similar system in his workshop as early as the 1860s (see Figs. 89 and 95); however, no explanation of this system has survived. One mark – a dot between the lion rampant and the sovereign's head of Hendery – which is found on flatware, can be identified with Walter Frederick Denman (Fig. 97).[10] But not all Hendery workmen had their own mark, and such was the case for John Leslie.[11] As for the Birks notched marks in Table 1, they are to be read in conjunction with any adjacent marks, exactly in the sequence in which they appear. For example, the marks on a piece made by John J. Walsh in 1905 would read: BIRKS STERLING (both incuse) followed by a fleur-de-lis-like notch which is upright – as seen in figure 98.

95

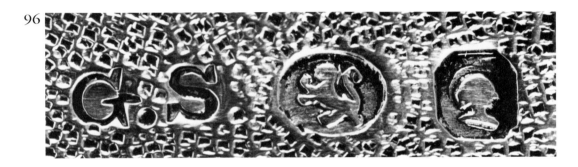

96

97

98

95 Marks on kiddush goblet (Fig. 42) by Robert Hendery & Co., c.1869. Birks (24137).

96 Marks on goblet (Fig. 71) by Robert Hendery for Gustavus Seifert, c.1864. Birks (25140).

97 Marks on teaspoon by Walter F. Denman as workman for Hendery & Leslie, c.1887–99. Birks (25509).

98 Marks on three-handled cup (Fig. 75) by John J. Walsh as workman for Henry Birks & Sons, 1905. Birks (25242).

Table 1 Identification marks of silversmiths employed in the silver factory of Henry Birks & Sons, from 1899 to 1935.

Silversmith	Mark	Dates
Thomas Allen Sr	A	1916–1920
Albert Maysenhoelder	O	1916–1928
Alphonse J. Dubé	D	1916–1935
Lawrence B. Morrison	M	1916–
J.A. Dunberry	Y	1916–1935
James McGrail	G	1916–1930
C. Taylor	T	1916–1930
W. Woodcock	W	1916–1920
	*	1920–
S. Brown	B	1916–
Albert Dumouchel Sr	BIRKS	1899–1900
Arthur W. Richards	BIRKS	1901–1933
C.B. Denman	♣	1901–1910
John J. Walsh	BIRKS ♣ STERLING	1901
	BIRKS ♣ STERLING	1902
	BIRKS ♣ STERLING	1903
	BIRKS ♣ STERLING	1904
	BIRKS STERLING ♣	1905
	BIRKS STERLING ♣	1906
	BIRKS STERLING ♣	1907
	BIRKS STERLING ♣	1908
	BIRKS ♣ STERLING	1909
	BIRKS ♣ STERLING	1910
	BIRKS ♣ STERLING	1911
	BIRKS ♣ STERLING	1912
	BIRKS STERLING ♣	1913
	BIRKS STERLING ♣	1914
	BIRKS STERLING ♣	1915
	BIRKS STERLING ♣	1916

BIRKS STERLING

1898	a			1901	d
1899	b			1902	e
1900	c			1903	f

1904-1924 BIRKS STERLING

1925	🦁Ⓘh	1945	Ⓐ🦁K	1966	Ⓐ🦁K
1926	🦁Ⓘi	1946	Ⓐ🦁L	1967	Ⓐ🦁l ✡
1927	🦁Ⓘm	1947	Ⓐ🦁M	1968	Ⓐ🦁l
1928	🦁Ⓘn	1948	Ⓐ🦁N	1969	Ⓐ🦁l
1929	🦁Ⓘo	1949	Ⓐ🦁O		
1930	🦁Ⓘp	1950	Ⓐ🦁P	1970	Ⓐ🛡n
1931	🦁Ⓘq	1951	Ⓐ🦁Q	1971	Ⓐ🛡o
1932	🦁Ⓘt	1952	Ⓐ🦁R	1972	Ⓐ🛡p
1933	🦁Ⓘs	1953	Ⓐ🦁S	1973	Ⓐ🛡q
1934	🦁Ⓘt	1954	Ⓐ🦁T	1974	Ⓐ🛡r
1935	⊙🦁Ⓘu	1955	Ⓐ🦁U	1975	Ⓐ🛡s
1936	🦁ⒶA	1956	Ⓐ🦁a	1976	Ⓐ🛡t
		1957	Ⓐ🦁b	1977	Ⓐ🛡u
1937	Ⓐ🦁B	1958	Ⓐ🦁c	1978	Ⓐ🛡A
1938	Ⓐ🦁C	1959	Ⓐ🦁d		
1939	Ⓐ🦁D	1960	Ⓐ🦁c	1979	Ⓔ🛡B
1940	Ⓐ🦁E	1961	Ⓐ🦁f	1980	Ⓔ🛡C
1941	Ⓐ🦁F	1962	Ⓐ🦁g	1981	Ⓔ🛡D
1942	Ⓐ🦁G	1963	Ⓐ🦁h	1982	Ⓔ🛡E
1943	Ⓐ🦁H	1964	Ⓐ🦁i	1983	Ⓔ🛡F
1944	Ⓐ🦁I	1965	Ⓐ🦁k	1984	Ⓔ🛡G

Table 2   Marking system for silver made by Henry Birks & Sons from 1898 to 1984. *Note:* the earliest date letters – that is, those for 1898 to 1901 – may actually have been applied to silver made by Hendery & Leslie for Henry Birks & Sons from *1896* until 1899.

As indicated by Table 2 (p. 103), in 1898 Birks introduced a system of date letters that was relatively short-lived. These letters were struck together with BIRKS (incuse), a sovereign's head in a square with clipped corners, and a lion rampant in an oval, the latter two acquired in 1899 as part of the Hendery legacy. By way of example are the marks on a tea tray (25308) in the Birks Collection, which include the letter d supposedly for 1901 (Fig. 99). Yet, as discussed in Chapter VI, the inscription and newspaper articles allude to this tray as a gift for a wedding that took place in the spring of 1899. A key to the resolution of this discrepancy must somehow lie in the fact that the early Birks date letters actually imitate nearly contemporary ones of the London (England) Assay Office, which was certainly the case for the Birks letters from 1925 to 1965. As d was the London date letter for 1899–1900 – that is, from May 1899 to May 1900 – this period could serve as a terminus post quem for the same Birks date letter. This proposition is entirely in accord with what we know about the tea tray, as it was supposed to have been finished in the summer of 1899. If the Birks d does signify 1899–1900, Ramsay Traquair must certainly be correct when he suggests that these letters were adopted by Birks as early as 1896, when Birks silver was still being made by Hendery & Leslie.[12] It follows that the letter d was probably used from 1899 until 1903, and not from 1901 until 1903 as shown in Table 2.

From about 1904 to 1924, Birks silver is most often struck with the marks BIRKS STERLING (both incuse), or simply BIRKS, and is frequently accompanied by marks as illustrated in Table 1. During this period, Roman Catholic Church plate continued to be marked with the lion rampant and sovereign's head of Hendery & Leslie, or close variants thereof. In 1925 date letters were reintroduced, this time in direct imitation of the cycle of the London Assay Office. Accompanying pseudo-hallmarks are a lion passant gardant and a wheat sheaf. In 1937 the sheaf was replaced by a letter C enclosing a lion's head erased, which was the Canadian national mark for silver. This mark signified that the article was made in Canada, and that it had a silver purity of 92.5 per cent, which was in conformity with the English Sterling standard. Figure 100 shows sample marks for 1946 as they appear on a tray

99

100

(25310). Two later changes should be noted. From 1970 onwards the lion becomes a lion sejant gardant, and from 1979, the national mark is the letter C enclosing a maple leaf.

Notes

1. Culme, *Nineteenth-Century Silver*, p. 5.
2. Langdon, *Guide to Marks*, p. 72.
3. Ibid., p. 73 (see illustration at bottom of page).
4. Ibid., p. 72.
5. While I refer to these two pseudo-hallmarks as belonging to Peter Bohle, the possibility does exist that they actually represent some kind of working association of Bohle and Robert Hendery. For example, the lion passant gardant was later used by Bohle & Hendery when in partnership, and in the late 1850s by Hendery alone. See note 6.
6. The absence of early marks identifiable with Hendery may indeed be due to the fact that he did not have need for any. A logical conjecture might be that he worked *for* rather than *with* Bohle in his early years, through the 1840s, before the two entered into partnership, with Hendery ultimately succeeding to the business in about 1856. That is not an unfamiliar progression.
7. "The work reflects great credit upon the manufacturer, — M. Hendry [*sic*], Craig Street..." *Montreal Gazette*, 6 Oct. 1859, p. 2.
8. For a complete list of retailers supplied by Hendery, and their marks, see Langdon, *Guide to Marks*, pp. 95–104; and J.E. Langdon, *Canadian Silversmiths 1700–1900* (Toronto: Privately Printed, 1966), pp. 224–228.
9. Culme, *Nineteenth-Century Silver*, pp. 24, 121.
10. National Gallery of Canada, Curatorial Archives, Notes of W.F. Denman, February 1939.
11. Langdon, *Canadian Silversmiths* (1960), p. 162.
12. R. Traquair, *The Old Silver of Quebec* (Toronto: Macmillan Company of Canada, 1940), p. 76.

Appendix II　　The Hendery & Leslie Silver Factory in 1894

The following extracts provide an exceptional glimpse of the internal organization and operations of the Hendery & Leslie silver factory in 1894. Their source is a typescript document in the Curatorial Archives of the National Gallery of Canada. Apparently this document is based on an account which John J. Walsh, a workman with both the Hendery & Leslie and the Birks firms, related to Henry G. Birks sometime in the early 1940s. For our purpose here, it seemed advisable to abridge the text somewhat. The introductory section, dealing with the Hendery predecessors, contains many factual errors and is evidently based on oral tradition. The concluding paragraphs about the later Birks factory are also of peripheral interest. In spite of these exclusions, the greater portion of the document is reproduced here. It has been annotated and some slight changes have been made to the paragraphing.

In 1894 when I started, there were about 20 employees. The old factory was situated on the West side of St. Peter St., No. 134, betwen Craig St. and Fortification Lane. The number is now 758 and the premises are now [early 1940s] occupied by United Photographic Stores and also Office Equipment Co. The factory occupied both floors in this two-story building; it must have been, at one time, a dwelling house. There was no basement.

The lower floor, on street level, was about 800 square feet in area. The upper floor was larger and ran South to Fortification Lane, and covered an area of about 2000 square feet. Part of the lower floor at the corner of Fortification Lane, was occupied by ''Adams'' an engraver and illuminator.[1] This accounted for the difference in area of the two floors.

The heating was done by coal stoves. Part of the duties of an apprentice was to tend the stoves and shovel in the coal, which was dumped on the sidewalk, as well as the coke which we used in the melting furnaces. In cold weather I went down on Sundays to stoke up the fires so the place would not be too cold on Monday morning.

On the lower floor was a small office, with a desk, presided over by Mr. Gore. On this floor was also done the plating in an area about 6' × 8' facing St. Peter St. The gold plater, Alfred Desroches,[2] had two jars each holding about one-half pint of gold plating solution. The silver plater, Dolphus Archambault,[3] son-in-law of A. Desroches, had two crocks, each holding about 5 gallons of silver plating solution.

The plating, both gold and silver, was originally done by energy produced by sal-ammoniac batteries. About 1895 this system of plating was changed with the installation of a small electric dynamo, to supply the required energy, also rheostats and other necessary equipment on a small scale.

The flatware shop was on the ground floor, at the back, or West side. The silver spoons and forks were all hammered (forged) by hand. Annealing was done in an open coke fire. The only piece of machinery used in the flatware shop was a small drop hammer, manually operated. This hammer weighed about 35 lbs., and was used to form the bowl of the spoon. One dozen ''Fiddle'' pattern tea spoons, hand forged and filed up, ready for polishing, was considered a good day's work for a spoonmaker.

I spent a short time, about 3 months, in the flatware department under Walter Denman,[4] who was foreman. There were two other spoonmakers, Alexandre David and C. Charbonneau.

Personnel, Old Shop 1894

Lower Floor

Mr. B. Gore	Book-keeper
Alfred Desroches	Gold Plater[5]
Dolphus Archambault	Silver Plater
Walter Denman	Flatware Shop Foreman
Alexandre David	Flatware maker
C. Charbonneau	Flatware maker

Upper Floor

Mr. John Leslie	Owner & Manager
Albert Dumouchel[6]	Silversmith Foreman
Albert Maysenhoelder[7]	Silversmith
Fred Fryer [Frier]	Silversmith
Alphonse Dubee [Dubé][8]	Silversmith
Con. Denman[9]	Silversmith
P. Giguere [Giguère]	Silversmith Apprentice
J.J. Walsh[10]	Silversmith Apprentice
H. Gaudry	Silversmith Repairman
A. Vincent[11]	Burnisher
Gus. Chagnon[12]	Burnisher
	also two flatware polishers

Until about 1896 Mr. Leslie did all the chasing as well as the designing. In that year we got a Scotchman, named David Angus, who was a pretty good chaser. In 1898 Angus got married and soon after left the shop....

Equipment

The power to drive the machines on the upper floor of the "Old Shop" came from the shafting in the printing plant of the "Daily Witness". This daily paper was issued by the "Witness Printing & Publishing Co." owned and operated by John Dougall.

The printing plant was at the back, or West side, of the Silver Shop, with an area-way, or yard, about 30 feet wide, between. A leather driving belt, about 14″ wide, came from the shafting in the printing plant, through a wooden box, 30 feet long, and drove a counter-shaft in the Silver Shop, from which the machines operated. This manner of operating the machines was far from satisfactory and eventually, about 1897, a motor was bought and installed in the Silver Shop to give us our own power, doing away with the long belting coming across the yard.

The machines operated by power were: a small spinning lathe, 12″ swing; a polishing lathe; a set of square wire rolls (still in use); a pair of 4″ flat rolls (still in use); and a fan for use with the melting and annealing furnaces.

In addition we had a wire drawing machine manually operated (the steel draw plates still in use); a pair of round wire rolls for small wire, manually operated (still in use). We also had a pair of 8″ flat rolls, manually operated. These 8″ flat rolls had cross arms connected to the end of each roll. It required four men to operate these rollers when rolling heavy stock 8″ wide.

A hand operated screw press was used for stamping medals, principally. The base of this press was made from the bole of a tree and was 20″ in diameter and 24″ high, to the top of which were bolted the slides that guided the hammer that was raised or lowered by a screw which was turned by a steel bar, set horizontally across the top of the screw. This bar was about six feet long to each end of which was attached a solid iron ball, about 8″ in diameter. Two men, one at each end of this bar, would swing the iron balls with all their force and the screw would carry the hammer downward till it came in contact with the medal dies placed on the base; this caused considerable pressure at impact and about six or eight of these blows, with several anneals in between, would usually bring up the detail of the embossing on the medal. This press, while quite efficient in its way, was not a factory-made tool. It appeared to be a home-made job. The press was bought by Mr. Hendery at a sheriff's sale; it had been used by a group of counterfeiters who, before their arrest, were operating in the wood, back of the mountain, probably in the vicinity of what is now the Town of Mount Royal.

The first silver we got from Handy & Harman, New York, was in 1897. Previous to this time all the silver used was alloyed, melted and rolled in our own shop. Even the large blanks for trays 22″ and 24″ were hammered to size in the shop....

Notes

1. F. Adams & Co. (Francis and Richard W. Adams), general engravers and copperplate printers. Francis Adams was an Englishman by birth (born c.1830), and a professional engraver, who settled in Montreal by 1853. He is known to have done the engraving on some Hendery presentation pieces as early as 1858 (*Montreal Transcript*, 21 July 1858, p. 2). It is also of interest that the working addresses of Adams and Hendery from 1869 onwards, although changing from time to time, were in close proximity on St Peter Street. In 1880 they both moved to and shared the same building, where they were still found in 1894. It is plausible that this was planned. Could it reflect an agreed working arrangement, with Hendery farming out much of the needed engraving, whether inscriptions or ornament, to Adams, a specialist in that field? Was their proximity suggested by mutual convenience? Traditionally most silversmiths had recourse to the skills of professional engravers rather than engaging in such work themselves. It must be added that in his earlier years of operation, at least, Hendery is also known to have used other engravers – for example, Thomas Ireland. Of course, if a piece of silver were a stock item rather than custom-made, an inscription could always have been added by anyone after it left the factory.
2. Desroches was a rather well-known amateur numismatist. At the beginning of his career he was listed in Montreal city directories as a jeweller, and, likely beginning sometime in 1859, he had a brief partnership with Francis Bohle until the latter's death 24 February 1860. Desroches later went to work for Hendery. He married Philomène Biron, the widow of the silversmith George David Bohle, in 1874.
3. Dolphus Archambault began working for Hendery & Leslie in 1891 and continued in the silver factory under Henry Birks & Sons Limited until 1938. He died 8 March 1941.
4. Walter Frederick Denman, son of the silversmith William Henry Denman. Born in 1857, he evidently worked for Hendery for a number of years.
5. At this period Desroches was regularly listed in Montreal city directories as a silversmith.
6. Born in 1860, Albert Dumouchel was apprenticed to Robert Hendery on 5 November 1874. He continued in the silver factory, later under Birks, retired in 1930, and died 4 August 1940.
7. Albert Maysenhoelder was related to (a son of ?) the silversmith David Maysenhoelder.
8. Alphonse J. Dubé began working for Hendery & Leslie in 1892, continued in the silver factory under Birks, and retired in 1939. He died 27 December 1940.
9. Charles Denman. He was the uncle of Walter Denman.
10. John J. Walsh began working for Hendery & Leslie in 1894, and continued in the silver factory under Birks.
11. Alexandre Vincent was listed in the 1892–93 Montreal city directory as a silverplater.
12. Gustave Chagnon was customarily listed in Montreal city directories as a silverplater.

Appendix III   List of Works in the Exhibition

Canadian Presentation Silver from the Henry Birks Collection

The National Gallery of Canada's exhibition of eighty-two presentation pieces from the Henry Birks Collection of Canadian Silver went on tour in March 1984, beginning 1 March to 30 April at the Vancouver Centennial Museum. The remainder of the exhibition schedule was as follows: Rivière-du-Loup, Quebec, Centre culturel du Bas-Saint-Laurent (1–30 June 1984); Moncton, New Brunswick, Moncton Museum (1 September–31 October 1984); Fort Smith, Northwest Territories, Northern Life Museum (1–31 December 1984); Calgary, Alberta, Nickle Arts Museum (15 January–15 February 1985); St Catharines, Ontario, Rodman Hall Arts Centre (3–31 March 1985); Peterborough, Ontario, Art Gallery of Peterborough (15 April–15May 1985); Sault Ste Marie, Ontario, Algoma Art Gallery (1–30 June 1985).

All works in the exhibition are from the Henry Birks Collection. Pieces are listed by maker, or by retailer if the maker is not known. The latter exceptions are always indicated. All works in the list, except those marked by an asterisk, are discussed in the text of this book. The following general information is provided for each: National Gallery accession number; former Birks accession number (if any); medium, dominant dimension; and the numbers of any relevant illustrations that appear in the book. These abbreviations are used: d. (diameter), h. (height), 1. (length), s. (silver).

Laurent Amiot
(Quebec City   1764–1839   Quebec City)
Child's cup (24141)   s.   h. 7.5 cm
Birks Q526 (Fig. 11)
Ecuelle with cover (24015)   s.   1. 29.7 cm
Birks Q324 (Fig. 12)

Andrew & Co., Ltd. (as retailer ?)
(active Winnipeg c.1901/05–1930)
Trowel (25145)   s. and ivory   1. 26.3 cm
Birks C361 (Fig. 79)

Henry Birks & Sons
(active Montreal from 1893)
Chalice (24032)   s.   h. 19 cm
Birks B64 (Fig. 77)
Credence paten with cover (27764)   s.   h. 11.3 cm
Birks B65 (Fig. 77)
Flagon (27763)   s.   h. 28 cm
Birks B63 (Fig. 77)
Inkwell (25244)   s. and hoof (equine)   1. 15.5 cm
Birks B97 (Fig. 76)
Punch bowl (24121)   s., gilt lined   1. 48.5 cm
Birks B141 (Fig. 78)
Tea tray (25308)   s.   1. 72.3 cm
Birks B79 (Figs. 74, 99)

Henry Birks & Sons
(active Montreal from 1893)
with John J. Walsh as workman
Three-handled cup (25242)   s. and horn   1. 26.4 cm
Birks B111 (Figs. 75, 98)

Peter Bohle
(Montreal   1786–1862   Montreal)
Mug (24086)   s.   h. 8.8 cm
Birks C645B (Figs. 9, 84)

Peter Bohle
(Montreal   1786–1862   Montreal)
for George Savage & Son
(active Montreal c.1825/28–1851)
Beaker (24078)   s.   h. 7.4 cm
Birks S118
Mug (25204)   s.   h. 9.5 cm
Birks S1 (Figs. 10, 85)

Bohle & Hendery
(active Montreal c.1851–1856)
for Savage & Lyman
(active Montreal 1851–1868)
Coffee pot (24125)   s. and ivory   h. 29 cm
Birks S88 (Figs. 20, 22, 91)
Cream jug (24123)   s., gilt lined   h. 13.8 cm
Birks S88 (Fig. 20)
Sugar bowl (24124)   s., gilt lined   h. 16.5 cm
Birks S88 (Fig. 20)
Teapot (24122)   s. and ivory   h. 24.5 cm
Birks S88 (Figs. 20, 21)

111

Cyrille Duquet
(Saint-Michel de Bellechasse, Que. 1841–1922 Quebec City)
Ceremonial key (25144)   s. 1. 16.7 cm
Birks Q329 (Fig. 56)

Elkington & Co.
(active London, England, 19th century)
and Hendery & Leslie (attributed)
(active Montreal 1887–1899)
Capital Lacrosse Club Cup (25136)   s., gilt lined h. 48.3 cm
Birks H133 (Fig. 73)

J.R. Harper & Co. (as retailer)
(active Montreal c.1873–1888)
Two-handled cup (24119)   s., gilt lined h. 14.2 cm
Birks H154 (Fig. 68)

Robert Hendery
(Corfu, Greece c.1814–1897 Montreal)
Mug (25198)   s., gilt lined h. 8.6 cm
Birks H263 (Fig. 94)
Porringer (25050)   s. 1. 24.3 cm
Birks H164 (Fig. 51)
*Trophy (25229)   s. h. 16 cm
Birks H108
*Wine goblet (27118)   s. h. 14.7 cm
*Wine goblet (27119)   s., gilt lined h. 14.9 cm

Robert Hendery
(Corfu, Greece c.1814–1897 Montreal)
for J.R. Harper & Co.
(active Montreal c.1873–1888)
Hunt Cup for 1882 of the Montreal Fox Hounds (24010)
   s., gilt lined   h.40.3 cm
Birks H63 (Fig. 67)

Robert Hendery
(Corfu, Greece c.1814–1897 Montreal)
for Savage & Lyman
(active Montreal 1851–1868)
Beaker (27757)   s., gilt lined h. 10.7 cm
Birks S114 (Fig. 50)
Child's cup (25208)   s. h. 11.9 cm
Birks S164 (Fig. 45)
Claret jug (27754)   s. h. 28.2 cm
Birks S72A (Figs. 32, 86)
Goblet (24138)   s. h. 19.2 cm
Birks S137 (Fig. 41)
Goblet (26098)   s., gilt lined h. 14.7 cm
(Fig. 33)
Goblet (26099)   s., gilt lined h. 14.6 cm
(Fig. 33)
Goblet (26100)   s., gilt lined h. 14.5 cm
(Fig. 33)
Goblet (26101)   s., gilt lined h. 14.5 cm

(Fig. 33)
Goblet (26102)   s., gilt lined h. 14.5 cm
(Fig. 33)
Goblet (26103)   s., gilt lined h. 14.4 cm
(Fig. 33)
Goblet (27755)   s. h. 18. 5 cm
Birks S72B (Fig. 32)
Goblet (27756)   s., gilt lined h. 18.5 cm
Birks S72B (Fig. 32)
Pitcher (25135)   s. h. 28.3 cm
Birks S131 (Fig. 36)
Pitcher (25139)   s. h. 34.5 cm
Birks S136 (Figs. 37, 38, 39)
Pitcher (26097)   s. h. 35 cm
(Figs. 33, 34, 35)
Tray (26104)   s. 1. 45.8 cm
(Figs. 33, 93)
Trophy (25147)   s. h. 9 cm
Birks S104 (Fig. 61)
Trophy (27759)   s. h. 18.5 cm
Birks S43B (Fig. 60)

Robert Hendery
(Corfu, Greece c.1814–1897 Montreal)
for Gustavus Seifert
(? 1831–1909 Quebec City)
Goblet (25140)   s. h. 20.8 cm
Birks H101 (Figs. 71, 96)

Robert Hendery
(Corfu, Greece c.1814–1897 Montreal)
for William H. Tracy
(active Ottawa c.1864–1892)
Trowel (25138)   s. and wood 1. 26 cm
Birks H74 (Fig. 54)

Robert Hendery
(Corfu, Greece c.1814–1897 Montreal)
for W.S. Walker
(active Montreal 1853–1892)
Road Race Cup of the Manitoba Turf Club (27752)
   s., gilt lined h. 29 cm
Birks H255 (Fig. 69)

Robert Hendery (attributed)
(Corfu, Greece c.1814–1897 Montreal)
for Savage, Lyman & Co.
(active Montreal 1868–1878)
Club Cup for 1872 of the Alexandra Snow Shoe Club (25237)
   s., gilt lined h. 17.5 cm
Birks S32 (Figs. 62, 89)

Robert Hendery & Co.
(active Montreal c.1866–1870)
*Goblet (25232)   s., gilt lined h. 17.6 cm

Birks H275
Kiddush goblet (24137)   s., gilt lined   h. 17.1 cm
Birks H215 (Figs. 42, 95)
Kiddush goblet (25134)   s., gilt lined   h. 17.1 cm
Birks H215 (Fig. 42)
Tray (24126)   s. 1. 40.6 cm
Birks H85 (Fig. 40)
Trophy (27761)   s., gilt lined   h. 19.4 cm
Birks H229 (Fig. 72)

Robert Hendery & Co.
(active Montreal c.1866–1870)
for Gustavus Seifert
(?   1831–1909   Quebec City)
Gallwey Tankard (25146)   s.   h. 17.7 cm
Birks H120 (Fig. 64)

Hendery & Leslie
(active Montreal 1887–1899)
with Albert Dumouchel as workman (attributed)
No. 2 Company Challenge Cup (25141)
    s., gilt lined   h. 17.8 cm
Birks H105
Railway spike (25143)   s. 1. 14 cm
Birks H46 (Fig. 55)

Hendery & Leslie
(active Montreal 1887–1899)
for Thomas Allan & Co.
(active Montreal c.1870)
Child's cup (25196)   s., gilt lined   h. 9.8 cm
Birks H20

Hendery & Leslie
(active Montreal 1887–1899)
for Gustavus Seifert
(?   1831–1909   Quebec City)
Trophy (25233)   s., gilt lined   h. 17.9 cm
Birks H72

J.G. Joseph & Co. (as retailer ?)
(active Toronto 1857–1878)
Challenge cup (25228)   s.   h. 19.9 cm
Birks C442 (Fig. 70)

Ambroise-Adhémar Lafrance
(Quebec City   1847–1905   Quebec City)
Child's cup (24087)   s., gilt lined   h. 8.3 cm
Birks Q77A (Fig. 49)
Mug (24084)   s., gilt lined   h. 7.6 cm
Birks Q77A

Lash & Co. (as retailer)
(active Toronto c.1871–1876)
Mug (25192)   s.   h. 8.3 cm

Birks C646 (Fig. 47)

Pierre Lespérance
(Quebec City   1819–1882   Quebec City)
Child's cup (27753)   s.   h. 6.6 cm
Birks Q129A (Fig. 48)

Salomon Marion
(Lachenaie, Que.   1782–1830   Montreal)
Goblet (24139)   s., gilt lined   h. 19.5 cm
Birks C4 (Fig. 4)

William Herman Newman
(Königsberg, Germany   1826–1894   Halifax)
The Nova Scotia Provincial Prize Cup (24230)
    s., gold, gilt lined   h. 41.5 cm
Birks M15 (Fig. 57)

Étienne Plantade
(Montreal   1777–1828   Montreal)
Snuffbox (27765)   s., gilt lined   1. 7.2. cm
Birks C2 (Fig. 5)

P. Poulin & Son (as retailer ?)
(active Quebec City c.1858–1875)
Trowel (25137)   s. 1. 30 cm
Birks U111 (Figs. 52, 53)

Frederick R. Reichel
(active San Francisco, California c.1856–1867)
Griffin Cup (24000)   s., gilt lined   h. 20 cm
Birks A84 (Fig. 59)

Roden Bros., Ltd.
(active Toronto c.1915–1953)
Two-handled cup with cover (25246)   s. gilt and wood
    h. 34.5 cm
Birks C251 (Fig. 80)

François Sasseville
(La Pocatière, Que.   1797–1864   Quebec City)
Beaker (27767)   s., gilt lined   h. 10.7 cm
Birks Q69A (Fig. 44)
Cruet tray (24146)   s. 1. 20.3 cm
Birks Q303 (Fig. 14)

Joseph Sasseville
(La Pocatière, Que.   1790–1837   La Pocatière, Que.)
Beaker (27789)   s.   h. 6.3 cm
Birks Q470

Savage & Lyman (as retailer)
(active Montreal 1851–1868)
Field Officer's Cup (24005)   s., gilt lined   h. 19.5 cm
Birks S107 (Fig. 58)

113

Fish fork (25968)   s.   l. 25.8 cm
Birks S89 (Fig. 43)
Fish slice (25967)   s.   l. 33.3 cm
Birks S89 (Figs. 43, 88)
Mug (25209)   s., gilt lined   h. 9.4 cm
Birks S163 (Fig. 46)
*Regiment Cup (25239)   s., gilt lined   h. 23.6 cm
Birks S92

Savage & Lyman (as retailer)
(active Montreal 1878–1885)
Annual Cup for 1880 of the Winnipeg Snow Shoe Club
  (25234)   s., gilt lined   h. 15.1 cm
Birks S145 (Figs. 63, 87)

Savage, Lyman & Co. (as retailer)
(active Montreal 1868–1878)
Muir Tankard (24117)   s. parcel-gilt, gilt lined
  h.27.2 cm
Birks S43A (Figs. 65, 66)
*Child's cup (25205)   s.   h. 9.6 cm
Birks S149

Nelson Walker
(Montreal   1799–after 1855   Great Britain)
Beaker (24118)   s., gilt lined   h. 10.7 cm
Birks C3 (Fig. 7)

Unidentified Maker
(active France, 19th century)
Paten (24148)   s.   d. 14.2 cm
Birks B64 (Fig. 77)

Selected Bibliography

Culme, John. *Nineteenth-Century Silver*. London: Country Life Books, 1977.

Gilbey, Walter. *Racing Cups 1559 to 1850*. London: Vinton & Co., 1910.

Ignatieff, Helena. "Canadian Presentation Pieces and Awards of Merit," *Canadian Collector*, XVI, 6 (Nov./Dec., 1981), pp. 40–42.

Klapthor, Margaret Brown. "Presentation Pieces in the Museum of History and Technology," *United States National Museum. Bulletin*, No. 241, pp. 83–107.

Langdon, John E. *Canadian Silversmiths 1700–1900*. Toronto: Privately Printed, 1966.

Mackay, Donald C. *Silversmiths and Related Craftsmen of the Atlantic Provinces*. Halifax: Petheric Press, 1973.

McClinton, Katharine Morrison. *Collecting American 19ᵗʰ Century Silver*. New York: Charles Scribner's Sons, 1968.

Nanavati, Tara Douglas. *Nineteenth Century Canadian Presentation Silver*. M.A. Thesis. Toronto: University of Toronto, 1977.

Wardle, Patricia. *Victorian Silver and Silver-Plate*. Foreword by Hugh Wakefield. London: Herbert Jenkins, 1963.

Index

Silver-makers' marks are shown in bold face type. Individual silver pieces are indexed, giving the name of collection in which the piece is held, the accession number, and the name of the maker or retailer. An *italicized page reference* indicates an illustration. Italics are also used in page references for individuals and organizations connected with a presentation piece – as in an inscription.

A list of presentation pieces under makers' names is given in Appendix III, pp. 111–114. Other makers whose works are illustrated in this book are indexed under "makers."